# Wellington

## JAMES HARDING

# The Duke of
# Wellington

by James Harding

INTERNATIONAL
PROFILES

# THE DUKE OF WELLINGTON
© James Harding, 1968

# INTERNATIONAL PROFILES
*General Editor:* EDWARD STORER

*English Language editions published in:*
GREAT BRITAIN, EUROPE AND SOUTH AMERICA
by Morgan-Grampian Books Limited,
28 Essex Street, Strand, London, W.C.2.

Republic of South Africa, Rhodesia and Malawi
by Nasionale Boekhandel Beperke,
Cape Town, Bloemfontein, Port Elizabeth and Johannesburg
Series Design: *Melvyn Gill.* Pictorial Research: *F. G. Thomas*
Covers: *Printed by George Over Limited, London and Rugby*
Paper: *Frank Grunfeld (Sales) Limited, London*
Text and Binding: *Hazell Watson & Viney Ltd., Aylesbury, Bucks*

# Author's Note

1. *Lt.-Col. The Hon. Arthur Wellesley*, c. *1795*. *(By permission of His Grace The Duke of Wellington.)*

In a book of this length it is impossible to cover the wide political, military and international issues raised by Wellington's unique career. The aim instead has been to draw a portrait of him as a man.

Wellington is the subject of innumerable anecdotes. Legendary though some of them may be – he did not, for example, say 'Up, Guards, and at 'em!' and neither did he claim that Waterloo was won on the playing fields of Eton – they have helped to create the English mystique. There are few areas of this country's public and social life which he did not influence and which, even today, do not carry the impress of his dominating personality. He has never ceased to excite the imagination of his compatriots, for whom he embodies so many of the qualities they like to think are theirs. One is tempted to adapt Voltaire and say that had Wellington not existed it would have been necessary to invent him.

A visit to the Duke's London home, Apsley House, now the Wellington Museum, can be a fascinating introduction to his life and times. The reader who wishes to follow the subject is invited to see the bibliography at the end of this book. Restricted though it is to works published in English, it is still only a very small selection out of many hundreds worth looking at. Let the reader be warned: an interest in the Duke of Wellington is apt to become a lifetime's passion.

2. *"Number One, London", Apsley House, Hyde Park Corner.*

# The Ugly Duckling

**1**  3. *Anne, Countess of Mornington.*  *(By permission of His Grace The Duke of Wellington.)*

Lady Mornington looked at the son whom she called her 'ugly boy Arthur' and sighed regretfully. What was to be done with him? At the age of sixteen he was a rawboned, unattractive lad. At school he showed little sign of cleverness, and in company he was timid and awkward. His mother thought hard about the problem and at last the answer came to her. He was, she decided, 'fit food for powder', and so, despite his rather frail constitution, a career in the army was chosen for him.

Things might have gone differently if his father had still been alive. The Earl of Mornington was an amiable and cultured nobleman whose family, of Rutland origins, had settled in Ireland a few centuries before. Life was pleasant for the Anglo-Irish aristocracy to which the earl belonged. They moved gracefully on a round of social enjoyment in a setting of well-kept parks and elegant mansions. In that pampered society the earl was noted for his lavish parties. He spent money with a generous hand and was continually 'improving' his estate. The ornamental lake was enlarged, canals were dug, and handsome rows of trees were planted. As the view from his window became grander, so his funds went on steadily diminishing.

The earl was also an accomplished musician. From an early age he had played the organ and violin with skill. As his gifts developed he turned to composing as well and wrote a great deal of music. In Dublin he founded a musical academy, and later he achieved eminence as Professor of Music, no less, at Trinity College. His sixth child was born on May Day, 1769, in the family's Dublin home at 24 Upper Merion Street. The boy, to be called Arthur, came into a household that resounded to the airs and glees which the happy father had composed. But Arthur was to know little of the easy life which the Morningtons had been brought up to regard as their right. The earl was already deep in financial trouble, and his extravagant tastes had led him so heavily into debt that he was reduced to buying lottery tickets in the desperate hope of restoring his fortunes. Three months after Arthur first saw the light of day, the Buonaparte family celebrated the birth of a son in distant Corsica.

Soon the Morningtons had left Ireland and set up house in London. Life was cheaper at their modest lodgings in Knightsbridge, where the earl, not long afterwards, died suddenly at the age of forty-five. He left a widow, seven children, and a mountain of debt. The title went to his eldest boy, Richard, who came down from Oxford to take charge of the struggling family. There is no doubt that he was Lady Mornington's favourite son. Practical, businesslike and purposeful, he brought order back into the Mornington's affairs. Richard it was who raised funds by negotiating mortgages on the Irish estate and settled debts after complicated transactions with creditors. At the same time he started to make a name for himself as a politician in the Irish House of Lords. His brother Arthur, then a shy twelve-year-old, could hardly be expected to emulate his brilliant elder. It was clear that Richard was the family hope. Arthur, meanwhile, went to school in Chelsea where the fees were low. Then came Eton, which he left after two years because his poor showing as a scholar did not justify the expenditure of money that could ill be spared.

Arthur was a quiet, lonely boy who missed his father. His mother he found unsympathetic. He knew she had a poor opinion of him, and this only served to drive him further into his sullen silence. After Eton she took him to Brussels, again in search of cheaper living conditions. There he studied for a year with a private tutor. The only talent he showed was for playing the violin, and like his father before him he began to take a deep interest in music. Much of his time he spent staring bleakly into the streets of Brussels, or comforting himself with the mournful tones of his violin. Apart from music, he was attracted by arithmetic and mechanical inventions. He often declared in later years that he would have liked to be a financier. None of this was calculated to soothe Lady Mornington's worries. She probably viewed his musical leanings as a dangerous inheritance of the unworldly tendencies which had ruined her husband. The family had suffered enough from such artistic nonsense. When Arthur was sixteen and 'fit food for powder', she sent him to a military academy at Angers, in France. At least, she reasoned, he would be able to learn a useful trade.

Arthur had never shown the slightest talent or wish for a soldier's career. The thought of entering the army had not even crossed his mind. It was easier to give way than to argue, so he did as he was told and set himself to master the secrets of this strange craft. As a matter of fact, Angers turned out to be the pleasantest school he ever attended. He learned to speak French with a good accent and to write it correctly. At an impressionable age he acquired from the local gentry Gallic notions of taste, manners and social conduct which transformed him from a raw lout into a polished young gentleman. Yet on the whole he still preferred his own company. Someone who knew him at the time remembered that he was quite happy to lie alone for hours 'on a sofa playing with a white terrier'.

He came back to England in 1787 and his mother looked at him with new eyes. His year abroad had certainly done something for her clumsy boy. She and his brother Richard busied themselves pulling strings on his behalf, and a few months before his eighteenth birthday he was gazetted an ensign in a Highland Regiment. The army into which Arthur Wellesley drifted was a peculiar institution. The men who filled its ranks were brutal, illiterate and vicious. They were treated like animals and mercilessly flogged at the slightest provocation. 'The scum of the earth' was how the future Duke of Wellington is said later to have described them, adding that they joined up for 'nothing but drink'. Yet at the time he first knew the army no-one attempted to improve the soldiers' miserable existence, and it was not surprising that they deserted whenever the opportunity arose. All the pleasures and rewards of army life were reserved for the nobility from whose ranks came the officers. Commissions were bought and sold. There were no proper examinations or training, and the only chance of promotion was through influence and money. At the top of this crazy structure sat the foolish man whose incompetence has been immortalized in the famous rhyme:

> The rare old Duke of York,
> He had ten thousand men,
> He marched them up to the top of the hill,
> And he marched them down again . . .

An ensign's pay of only £125 a year was small enough for a young man of limited prospects, and once again brother Richard came to the rescue by arranging for him to be appointed aide-de-camp to the Lord Lieutenant of Ireland. His regiment being conveniently away on foreign service, Arthur returned once again to the city of his birth. Dublin society was charmed by his elegant figure in the handsome red uniform and the dandy's neatness which earned him the nickname of 'the Beau'.[1] He went to parties, was sought after by the ladies, ran political errands for the Lord Lieutenant, and in between times he still played languishing tunes on the violin. Sterner duties were on the way, and before he was twenty-one the helpful Richard had engineered him into sitting as MP for Trim in the Irish Parliament. It was his first taste of politics, and although, with his usual seriousness, he made himself learn all he could about his new job, he never conquered a basic dislike for democratic assemblies where everything depended on unreliable majorities and shifting allegiances, rather than on a straightforward chain of military command.

Gradually he rose in the army. He became a lieutenant soon after joining and was a captain by the time he was twenty-two.

[1] He only heard of the nickname many years later, at the age of forty-two. 'Well! by God,' he remarked mildly, 'I never knew I was a beau before.'

4. *Kitty Pakenham.*   *(By permission of the Mansell Collection.)*

In 1793 a loan from the sale of the family estates enabled him to buy a commission as a major, and, within several months, as a lieutenant-colonel. This rapid ascent was the result of no passing whim. He had by now made up his mind to concentrate on his career. There was, too, a girl called Kitty Pakenham who took up quite a lot of his attention. How could he support a wife unless he found success in his profession? Henceforward he put behind him the pleasures of cards and the gay parties at Dublin Castle. More difficult still was the resolution he made to give up his beloved violin. But he carried it out. One day he grasped the instrument that had been the only comfort of so many lonely hours and pitched it grimly on the fire. He never spoke about it afterwards.

While Lieutenant-Colonel Wellesley immersed himself with new determination in problems of drilling and strategy, across the water in France Louis XVI was tumbled from his throne and revolution flamed throughout the country. The old order was smashed. The new men who rose from out of the chaos were, in their turn, murdered on guillotines slippery with blood. The turmoil spread over Europe, and soon an unwilling England, already exhausted by other recent wars, found herself and her allies grappling with a huge Revolutionary Army. The tide of war crashed into the Netherlands, where the grand old Duke of York and an expeditionary force had been sent to defend the country. In fact, however, they were engaged in a desperate retreat. Lieutenant-Colonel Wellesley and his regiment were ordered to join them at Ostend. They were greeted by an army largely made up of ex-convicts, raw young recruits and decrepit old men; it was staffed by untrained officers and attended by a medical corps of drunken apothecaries and failed doctors. The retreat of this disorganized rabble was interrupted momentarily at the little village of Boxtel, in Brabant. It was here that Wellesley fought his first battle. He ordered his men to hold their fire until the oncoming French were nearly level with them. Suddenly, at his command, a thunderous volley broke out and sent the enemy reeling back. But it was only a temporary respite, and the English went on retreating through the gloomy autumn days until they ended up by the river Waal.

A harsh winter set in. Through the frozen night the lights of the French camp glittered on the opposite bank of the Waal, and by day scores of black figures flitted across the sharp white snow. The weather was so bad, Wellesley thought, that they would not attack.

He was wrong. The temperature fell still lower, the river iced up, and before January was out the French came storming across the jagged floes. The weary retreat staggered on leaving a train of dead men and horses, shattered carts and heaps of equipment that the remorseless snow began steadily to envelop. Of the twenty-five thousand men who had begun the campaign, only six thousand now struggled exhausted into the port of Bremen on the way home.

The one distinguished feature of this otherwise appallingly managed operation was the stand Wellesley had made at Boxtel. Whatever else the campaign brought about, it had at least given him a practical though bitter apprenticeship. 'It has always been a marvel to me how any one of us escaped,' he said afterwards. He had seen for himself the results of bad planning and the disasters that came from poor administration. He never forgot the importance of properly organized communications and the need for regular supplies of food and equipment. 'The real reason why I succeeded in my own campaigns is because I was always on the spot,' he explained. 'I saw everything, and did everything for myself.' When someone asked him if his experiences in Holland had been of use to him, he summed up the matter with his curt reply: 'Why, I learnt what one ought not to do, and that is always something.'

5. *Garret Wellesley, 1st Earl of Mornington.* *(By permission of His Grace The Duke of Wellington.)*

# India

6. *The Castle at Gawilghur.*   (*By permission of the India Office Library.*)

## 2

He was an ugly duckling no longer. A colleague described him at this time as '. . . all life and spirits. In height he was about five feet seven inches, with a long, pale face, and remarkably large aquiline nose, a clear blue eye, and the blackest beard I ever saw. He was remarkable clean in his person, and I have known him shave twice in one day, which, I believe was his constant practice. . . . He spoke at this time remarkably quickly, with, I think, a very, very slight lisp. . . .' But the Dublin to which he returned had little to offer 'the Beau'. More than a year went by in writing polite letters and seeking interviews with important people likely to help him find a well-paid post that would enable him to clear off his mounting debts. For once even Richard's influence was unsuccessful. Inactivity weighed heavily on the young lieutenant-colonel. His depression grew as he saw his hopes of command dwindle slowly away.

Then, in the middle of 1796, he was ordered to India. Perhaps higher authority, wearied of his pestering, had decided that a foreign posting was a convenient way of getting rid of this importunate officer. As if to compensate for the unhealthy tropical climate for which he was destined, a further promotion brought him a colonelcy. He was unabashed at the prospect of serving in a country which, only too often, turned out to be a graveyard both physical and mental. It at least gave him an opportunity for the action which his new-found ambition had been hungering after for several years. He resigned his parliamentary seat, and by the end of June a frigate was bearing him off to Calcutta. Whatever may have been the intention of his superiors in sending him abroad, Colonel Wellesley had determined to make the very best of the situation. For a journey that was to last over six months he took with him several trunks full of books for reading on the voyage. While a gusty sea wind filled out the white sails and twanged at the rigging, he sat below in his cabin and worked through a demanding course of study. The history of India and accounts of military campaigns fought there absorbed much of his attention. Other topics included the various dialects of India, its commerce, geography and administration. Neither did he neglect to instruct himself on the legal and political aspects of Indian problems. It was a rigorous and exhausting way to educate himself – but when he landed at Calcutta in February he was probably the best informed traveller of his time to set foot there.

The British East India Company had been active in the country since the seventeenth century. At the time of Wellesley's arrival it administered a sprawling empire which covered Bombay, Madras and Bengal. These three presidencies were under the rule of a British Governor-General. The empire had been established over the years by the efforts of a surprisingly small number of venturesome pioneers, and it was carried on by an equally small group of businessmen and administrators. Scattered about the land were many native states with whom the British lived on terms that ranged from uneasy peace to outright war. The presence of an army was, therefore, a permanent necessity to safeguard the commercial well-being of the Company.

The men who came out to India and succeeded made vast fortunes. They lived with a luxury they could not have afforded at home, and they built for themselves magnificent houses which were staffed by throngs of servants. If they were lucky enough to escape the tropical fevers which, just before Wellesley's arrival, had killed, in one month alone, seventy European residents in Calcutta, then life could be very agreeable indeed. The Anglo-Indians ate, drank and entertained with a lavishness which recalled the Anglo-Irish of Wellesley's childhood. Their supper dances went on until dawn and their hangovers tended to last for as much as forty-eight hours at a time. The serious-minded Colonel Wellesley did not find much to attract him about their behaviour. He preferred a plate of cold mutton to their interminable dinners at which every conceivable variety of meat and fish and game was eagerly gormandized. He could eat rancid butter and bad eggs, as he was often to do on later campaigns, and notice nothing wrong. He drank wine hardly at all. It may have been his involuntarily austere way of life at this time that preserved his good health. Strangely enough, the place suited him very well. Where other men's constitutions might be undermined by the steamy heat, Wellesley seemed to thrive on it. He even contrived to throw off the last trace of youthful ailments which had dogged him up to then. His morale was good and he was able to bear with patience the indifference of officialdom and the obstruction by jealous superior officers which he had become used to facing. As he went about his duties under the waving palm trees and past the straggling bamboo groves, he could not help feeling that life at last was beginning to favour him.

His optimism was encouraged when he heard that Richard had been appointed Governor-General of India. One hot May morning he rode down to meet his brother off the ship and to see him installed amid great pomp in a splendid palace. Richard, now a baron, was fond of display, partly because he loved to show off his own importance and partly because he knew that grandeur was a useful aid to diplomacy. He was quick to appreciate Arthur's wide knowledge of Indian affairs and soon formed an effective partnership with him. From then on Richard looked to Arthur for the unofficial advice he could rely upon. The two brothers between them tackled and solved the problems of an empty treasury and a much reduced army. More serious still was the growing menace of native States which, encouraged and assisted by France, were preparing for war. The strongest of the native rulers was Tippoo Sahib, whose army included many thousands of crack troops trained by the French. Richard was anxious to gain the advantage of surprise by attacking first. On this occasion it was the soldier who argued against war. Arthur advised delay until their own forces were built up and they could fight from a position of strength. He won his point against the warlike civilian. Diligently, patiently, he undertook the task of reorganizing a broken-down army. It was on such humdrum matters as supplies of grain, rounding up bullocks and allocating rations that he concentrated. His correspondence was full of references to such exotic tradesmen as 'sadawkers' and 'brinjarries' with whom he bargained for groceries and rice. His quick intelligence accounted for every detail, from the greasing of cartwheels to the provision of tobacco for the Indian troops. The lesson of the disastrous Holland expedition had been well digested.

There came a moment when diplomatic exchanges with Tippoo could keep the peace no longer. The war-hungry sultan unleashed his troops and embarked on his crusade to drive the British from India. Down in Madras, where Colonel Wellesley had his base, the army prepared to march. It was, as he himself admitted, 'a ponderous machine'. In the spring of 1799 he led it from Madras and up towards the highlands of Mysore, a lumbering, lurching procession of one hundred and twenty thousand bullocks carrying supplies, elephants loaded with equipment, donkeys and camels. Amid the bellowing, the braying and the groaning creak of heavy carts, this unwieldy host formed itself into a giant hollow square several miles across and rolled slowly through the countryside. It was accompanied by an army some forty thousand strong.

By the month of April they were encamped near Tippoo's capital of Seringapatam. 'Ponderous' the British arrangements might have been, but a clash between the two armies left them victorious. Wellesley's emphasis on the efficient organization of supplies and lines of communication was shown to be well placed. A few days later there followed a skirmish by night in a thick forest where men fought stumbling and cursing through clinging undergrowth. Wellesley himself was hit on the knee by a spent bullet and the advance was briefly checked. It was one of the rare defeats in his career. He became, an officer noted, 'Mad with this ill success'. He realized, too late, the rashness of attacking in the dark without previous reconnaissance. The memory of that bitter night rankled for many years. People who knew the 'Iron Duke' in later times believed, quite wrongly, that he had no nerves. They had never seen him as he was on the aftermath of his first defeat, grieving, haggard, and at last falling into an exhausted sleep on the mess table.

Next day the post was taken and Wellesley camped in siege around Tippoo's capital. A merciless bombardment made gaping holes in the wall. Men poured through it to fight in the streets. The town was theirs and they went mad with the desire for plunder, rioting through the smoking ruins and pillaging by the lurid fire of burning houses. Tippoo was found, dead, under a heap of carpets, and his green flag was torn down from his palace. Among his treasures the invaders discovered beautiful illuminated manuscripts in which the insane visionary had noted down his ambitious dreams. The precious velvet hanging which adorned his tent was carried off and may be seen today in the Wellington Museum. Hard though he tried, Wellesley never completely succeeded in stamping out the tradition of plunder which his soldiers always followed. Despite the half-dozen gallows he put up and the bodies that dangled from them in stark silhouette against the blue Indian sky, he had great trouble with the problem. He always contended that his men should be satisfied with the prize money that was handed out on these occasions. It was generous enough, for his own share amounted to seven thousand pounds, a sum that enabled him to settle his bills and to be free of debt for the first time in his life.

There was much for the thirty-year-old colonel still to do. He was appointed Governor of Mysore and succeeded in restoring order among the troops only by dint of much flogging and hanging. His leadership was needed to sort out the tangled state into which the civil administration had fallen, and here the months of study he had spent on the voyage to India bore fruit. The founding of a legal system and the rebuilding of Seringapatam were all his work. Agriculture, trade and commerce had their due of his attention, and even the resettlement of the ladies from Tippoo's harem was thoughtfully taken into account.

Fom time to time guerilla fighting broke out in the area. One very troublesome free-booter, who styled himself King of the Two Worlds, darted about ravaging the countryside and winning large numbers of followers. Wellesley set out with his usual cumbersome force, plodding through tangled jungles and over deep, fast-flowing rivers, while his mobile guerilla foe circled around and harassed him like a gad-fly. In the end Wellesley's perseverance told. A lightning cavalry charge with the Colonel at its head pinned down the elusive enemy, and the self-declared king was sent to what was presumably the second of his Two Worlds. The kindly Wellesley adopted his infant son who had been captured at the battle, paid for his keep and education, and arranged for him to have a good start in life.

The routine days went on in Seringapatam. After morning parade, when he gave his orders in cocked hat, long coat, white pantaloons and Hessian boots, Wellesley retired to his office and the never-ending flow of paper-work. One day there was a gleam of hope that he might be released from the daily chores of organizing drainage networks and policing bazaars. He had the possibility of an expedition to Ceylon to engage the French – but nothing came of it and he returned disconsolately, his hope of higher command dashed once again. Eagerly he sent for the latest promotion list. His name was not to be seen on it.

'*My highest ambition* is to be a *Major-General* in His Majesty's service,' he said longingly. He was now thirty-two and prematurely grey as the result of an attack of jungle fever. His fate, as he saw it, was to rot away in an obscure corner of India, while outside in the greater world his exact contemporary, Napoleon Bonaparte, ruled a nation and commanded an army. Both the East India Company and the War Office were grudging in their recognition of his work. Time and again he was forced to see men whom he knew to be incompetent promoted over his head. Disappointment even made him quarrel with his brother. At last, in 1802, when the April promotions raised him to Major-General, the move came too late to give him any real pleasure.

He revealed little of this to the people around him. He was already an adept at presenting a poker face. There was nothing he deplored more than demonstrativeness, and he had learned in a hard school the advisability of concealing what he felt. In his daily negotiations with Indian princes and peasants, with civilians

13

and with soldiers, he knew the value of keeping a cool head. Yet Wellesley only achieved his icy manner through stern self-control, and beneath the cold exterior he was as liable as any man to violent emotion.

He tried to forget his feelings in hard work. Richard, on the other hand, was glorying in the magnificence of his position and indulging to the full his taste for the spectacular. The Governor-General appeared in public to an accompaniment of drums and banners. He was attended by retinues of servants in bejewelled turbans and flowing robes, and his processions were enlivened with elephants bearing canopies of State. He even went so far as to enlarge his personal bodyguard to a band of four hundred men who strutted on sentry duty in the corridors of his palace. Within earshot of his brother's glittering parades, Major-General Wellesley toiled doggedly at the less glamorous business of reforming abuses, clearing jungles and building roads.

It became obvious in the last months of 1802 that a war with the Mahratta Confederacy would be necessary before the British could claim really to control India. Since the seventeenth century the Mahratta princes had lorded it over a great tract of country which ran the breadth of the continent and overlapped in many places with territories administered by the East India Company. The Mahratta armies amounted to over a quarter of a million men, including artillery and cavalry trained up to high standards by the French. Wellesley was ready for action when his brother decided the time was ripe to deal with this last remaining obstacle to British power in India. Once again he tackled the dull but essential job of organizing bullock trains, packing supplies and establishing a system of depots. By February of the following year the last keg of salt beef had been stowed away, the last sack of biscuits piled into the waggons and the 'ponderous machine' laboured cautiously over the rough Indian terrain. Every detail of organization had been supervised by its commander, even down to the exact speed at which it was to travel.

At the end of a hard day's march under the burning sun towards Poona, intelligence arrived that the town's Mahratta chief was threatening to destroy it. Leaving his weary infantry behind, Wellesley made a desperate dash with his cavalry and rode sixty miles through the night in time to forestall the plan. The enemy took fright at this sudden action, and as they fled out by one gate, Wellesley and his men, covered in dust but triumphant, galloped in by another. For the next few weeks Poona was the base where he negotiated interminably with the Mahratta envoys for an end to hostilities. It was a trying period, for his antagonists played a waiting game and hoped to deceive him into withdrawal. His patience was equal to the task. So was his shrewdness. Scenting the Mahrattas' real purpose, he suddenly broke off negotiations and made a surprise attack on the supposedly impregnable fort of Ahmednuggar. The fort itself stood near the top of a hill, with a town clustered about its base and surrounded by a wall. Torrential rain beat fiercely down as the English made their preparations. Next morning the weather cleared, and the storming party swept up the ladders and were cutting their way through the defenders before anyone fully realized what had happened.

In all the excitement of battle, Wellesley never for a moment lost sight of administrative detail. He always found time to care about the food and welfare of his men, for, he said, 'I consider nothing in this country so valuable as the life and health of the British soldier'. On went the 'ponderous machine' under the watchful eye of its leader, deeper and deeper into the lands of the Mahrattas, vanishing into the black shadows of jungle and ravine to emerge suddenly into the dazzling sunlight of the plain. They came to a river swollen with yellow floods, and one by one the different sections were ferried across in stoutly constructed basket boats. 'In fact, we made war pretty much as Alexander the Great seems to have done,' said Wellesley, 'and as all men must do in such a country as India then was.' On a later occasion he remarked: 'I had *Caesar's Commentaries* with me in India, and learnt much from them, fortifying my camp every night as he did. I passed over the rivers as he did, by means of baskets and boats of basketwork. . . .'

They knew that somewhere in the neighbourhood the Mahratta army was lurking in great numbers. On September 23 Wellesley came upon them unexpectedly, near the village of Assaye. It was too late to cast about and fight in a place of his own choosing, so he made a perilous gamble by crossing what he rightly guessed to be a ford in the hope of out-manoeuvring the enemy. But the Mahrattas were not to be tricked, and the engagement that followed was among the hardest-fought India had ever seen. The Seventy-fourth Regiment was almost wiped out in Assaye, and Wellesley twice had his horse shot beneath him. After five hours of acrid combat, the bayonets of the Seventy-eighth at last dislodged the Mahrattas, who fled away leaving most of their arms and equipment behind them.

Assaye marked a decisive point in the Mahratta Wars. After resting his army, Wellesley caught up with the enemy and inflicted a short sharp defeat on them at Argaum. Now there only remained the fortress of Gawilghur to be stormed. Like Ahmednuggar, it was perched on a hill and surrounded by rugged country believed to make it inaccessible. Along roads hastily built by Wellesley's army, over mountains and through towering gorges, supplies and ammunition were laboriously dragged by hand. Gawilghur fell to a businesslike attack on December 15, and before the year was ended treaties had concluded the Mahratta Wars. India was at peace and British power was firmly established.

In Poona and Bombay Wellesley was greeted with flattering addresses and receptions in his honour. These he accepted in his usual cool and dignified way. What touched him most was the elaborate gold and silver plate which his officers gave him. It caused him more pleasure than the knighthood which the government conferred on him as tardy acknowledgement of the ablest commander they had. Pleasant though it was to know that authority was at last beginning to realize his worth, he could not help feeling a little bored. For months on end he had endured the monotony and discomfort of camp life, the nervous strain of incessant campaigning, and the steadily deteriorating effect of a treacherous climate. Though the life he led was temperate and he dined chiefly on rice – a dish which remained a favourite for the rest of his life – and drank little or no wine, his health was showing the strain. Rheumatism, ague and the Malabar itch plagued him intermittently, so that he looked, said a friend, 'sallow and wan, and with every mark of what is called a worn out man'. Far more significant to him than the flowery language of official proclamations was the approach of the rainy season and the attacks of rheumatism that inevitably accompanied it.

He did his work conscientiously and the stream of memoranda flowed unchecked from his pen. But his heart was not in it. He was restless. However many novels he read, however many women he flirted with, he could not prevent his thoughts from turning towards England. Early in 1805 an unwilling Richard accepted his resignation and he sailed for home through blustery weather and attacks of sea-sickness which failed to damp his good humour. He was leaving India, moreover, with a private fortune of thirty thousand pounds. Large though this was, it was still far smaller than what he might have made had he stooped to the corruption that traditionally enriched officials of the East India Company. Now the boat sailed on in gentler weather through the Atlantic. Presently an island rose out of the sea and he broke his journey to spend a leisurely three weeks exploring the 'beautiful' place. It had, he wrote with unconscious irony, a climate that was 'the most healthy I have ever lived in'. The name of the island was St Helena, and ten years later it was to be the scene of the last exile of his antagonist Napoleon.

7. *Asirgarh.* *(By permission of the India Office Library.)*

# Peninsular:
# First Phase

*(By permission of the National Portrait Gallery.)*

# 3

Sir Arthur's arrival in England was as quiet and muted as the weather on that autumn day in 1805 when he sailed into Portsmouth harbour. The directors of the East India Company, whose power he had done so much to consolidate, were loath to meet him, for his very success had made them jealous of him as a possible rival. Even the Secretary for War, to whom Sir Arthur reported on his return to London, kept him waiting for over an hour. In the ante-room where he cooled his heels he found himself with a one-armed gentleman who was also attending for an interview. The latter's conversation was '. . . so vain and so silly as to surprise and almost to disgust me,' recalled Sir Arthur. His astonishment was all the greater in that he had recognized his companion as Nelson. After a few minutes' talk Nelson left the room to enquire the name of the unknown military man who was with him. When he was told his manner changed completely, and on his return,

Sir Arthur noted '. . . I don't know that I ever had a conversation that interested me more.' A few weeks later Nelson was killed at the Battle of Trafalgar.

The ailing William Pitt was then Prime Minister, and Sir Arthur dined at the Guildhall on that historic occasion when Pitt made what must be the most effective short speech ever heard. 'Europe is not to be saved by any single man,' said he. 'England has saved herself by her exertions, and will, as I trust, save Europe by her example.' Sir Arthur was impressed. 'He was scarcely up two minutes,' he said, 'yet nothing could be more perfect.' Pitt would have been a good friend, as he had a high opinion of Wellesley. In January of the following year, however, he died, and Sir Arthur had to be content with the humble command of a brigade at Hastings. 'I am *nimmukwallah*, as we say in the East,' he would explain to friends who saw the appointment as a snub after his important Indian command, 'that is, I have ate of the King's salt, and, therefore, I conceive it to be my duty to serve with unhesitating zeal and cheerfulness, when and wherever the King or his government may think proper to employ me.'

This readiness to do his duty had an effect on his private life which can only be described as unfortunate. He was soon reunited with Kitty Pakenham, the girl whom he once thought to have loved. It was his infatuation for her that had made him think seriously of building a career in the army so that he might be able to support a wife and family. Now he was back with a knighthood, high rank and a fair-sized fortune. She was thirty-three and had waited patiently for his return. He no longer loved her. On arriving from India he had been horrified by the change in her appearance. Her pert round face had suddenly withered and her youthful, if fluttery charm, was replaced by gushing chatter. 'She is grown damned ugly, by Jove!' he whispered to a friend. She accepted his dutiful proposal with a shade too much eagerness, and in the spring of 1806 they were married at St George's Church, Dublin. Though she loved him and admired him, she was secretly afraid of him, and the fear he inspired in her only increased her nervous volubility. She knew she got on his nerves, so she rather pathetically turned a blind eye to his flirtations with other women and pretended not to be hurt by his obvious pleasure when official duties called him away from her. The most she could be sure of was that he would always treat her honourably. The birth of their first son helped matters a little. Though he may have been a reluctant husband, he was to prove an affectionate father.

In the meantime brother Richard had resigned his Governor-Generalship of India and come back to England. Almost immediately he became the subject of violent political attacks by enemies who hoped to impeach him as they had done with Warren Hastings. It was thought that his brother would be the obvious choice to defend him against his Parliamentary opponents, and Sir Arthur obligingly entered the House of Commons as member for Rye. His sympathies lay rather with the Tories than the Whigs, and after he had successfully vindicated Richard he continued his political career as the representative of a Cornish borough. He was not to be a back-bencher for long. A change of government put Richard's friends into power, and Sir Arthur was invited to serve as Chief Secretary for Ireland.

After the Irish rebellions of the previous century, Pitt had united the country with Britain and granted it representation in the English Parliament. He had failed, through the opposition of George III, to do away with the law that forbade Catholics to hold public office. This was a problem which, all unknown to Sir Arthur as he took up his new post in Dublin, was to haunt him twenty years later when he himself became Prime Minister. He had no illusions about his task. He knew the English held on to Ireland for military reasons and were detested as alien invaders. In his delicate handling of religious differences, political intrigues, and the dispensation of patronage, he drew heavily on his long experience of negotiating with devious Indian potentates. Surrounded by nagging disputes and swirling cross-currents of passion, he remained patient and realistic. There was, he reported to London, no political measure that '. . . would alter the temper of the people of this country. . . . Shew me an Irishman and I'll shew you a man whose anxious wish it is to see his country independent of Great Britain. . . .'

A brief but welcome respite from the cares of his Irish administration arose when he was again appointed to command an expeditionary force. This time it was to Copenhagen, where the British government had ordered him to capture the Danish fleet. Now Denmark was a neutral country, and this unusual move caused immense indignation. For once, however, the government showed admirable initiative. The fleet was a large one, and had Napoleon been able to take it himself it would have been a valuable aid to an invasion of England. The surprise nature of the attack, linked with impeccable planning, brought complete success. That the action had been the right one was proved by Napoleon's towering rage when he heard that the ships had been snatched from under his nose. Sir Arthur came back to his London home in Harley Street, taking with him a handsome horse which he promptly baptised 'Copenhagen'.

Among Sir Arthur's most useful gifts was that of being able to concentrate on one thing at a time and to keep his mind free of all that did not concern the topic of the moment. Immediately on his return he was deep in Irish affairs again and studying the problem of keeping order in Limerick with such absorption that Copenhagen might never have existed. This did not mean, though, that he was unaware of the events that were convulsing Europe. Like everyone else he had watched Napoleon sweep from success to success until it had seemed that the little Corsican was invincible. One of Napoleon's earliest and most dazzling victories had occurred in 1805 at Austerlitz, where the Austrians fell to the Emperor. In the following year the Prussians were routed at Jena. A few months later, at Tilsit, Napoleon signed an agreement with the Tsar which gained him the powerful friendship of Russia. England herself, though at Trafalgar she had asserted her naval supremacy, could not help but suffer from the effects of a blockade which the French were conducting with the aim of cutting off her supplies. And then, in 1807, Napoleon began to increase his pressure on Spain and Portugal. Ruled by a quavering monarchy and a feeble government, Spain had already been a compliant ally of France for over a decade, paying tribute to the Emperor of many millions of gold francs a year. After a bewildering series of plot and counter-plot, secret treaties and backstairs alliances, a French army of nearly one hundred thousand men sliced its way through Spain and captured the main fortress there. But the proclamation of Napoleon's brother Joseph as King of Spain was too much for the people of Madrid. They rose up and fought the French regiments in the streets of their city. Despite the fury with which they were massacred, their example was followed by revolts throughout the rest of the country. While Spain was being taken care of, Napoleon sent an expeditionary force into Portugal. It reached Lisbon to find that the Queen, her fleet and her treasury had, on the advice of the British ambassador, escaped and given Napoleon the slip.

In June, 1808, a representative of the Spanish authorities arrived in London to ask for help. Within a very few days the British government had agreed to give aid and drawn up its plans. The peninsula formed by the lands of Spain and Portugal would provide the long-awaited chance to engage the French in a fixed theatre of war. Instead of sending out expeditions to far-off skirmishes, it would at last be possible to hold down an elusive enemy and wage regular warfare. It is probable that the decision was influenced by Sir Arthur, now a Lieutenant-General, for the Cabinet had got into the habit of asking his opinion on all military matters and much besides – so much so, indeed, that he wryly called himself '. . . the *willing horse*, upon whose back every man thinks he has a right to put the saddle'. Inevitably, on June 14 he was placed in command of the Peninsular forces. He resigned his Chief Secretaryship and its eight thousand pound salary without a pang.

One evening in Harley Street, just before he left England, he entertained a colleague to dinner. After they had eaten, his thoughts seemed to be elsewhere, and he remained silent for so long that he was asked what he was thinking about. 'Why, to say the truth,' replied Sir Arthur, 'I'm thinking of the French that I am going to fight. I have not seen them since the campaign in Flanders, when they were capital soldiers, and a dozen years of victory under Bonaparte must have made them better still. They have besides, it seems, a new system of strategy, which has out-manoeuvred and overwhelmed all the armies of Europe. 'Tis enough to make one thoughtful; but no matter: my die is cast, they may overwhelm me but I don't think they will out-man-oeuvre me. First, because I am not afraid of them, as everybody else seems to be; and secondly, because if what I hear of their system of manoeuvres be true, I think it a false one as against steady troops. I suspect all the continental armies were more than half beaten before the battle was won. I, at least, will not be frightened beforehand.' Whereupon Sir Arthur went serenely to bed meditating the advantages of light infantry as against marauding

French sharpshooters, and the superiority of quickfiring squares over Napoleon's cavalry.

By the middle of July he was making his farewells of a tearful Kitty and embarking happily for Portugal. The only cloud on his horizon was the continued presence in authority of the ineffectual Duke of York. Even before Sir Arthur landed on the Portuguese beaches he heard that two of York's henchmen were to be put over him. One was Sir Harry Burrard, an ancient soldier whose record was one of unmitigated defeats. The other was Sir Hew Dalrymple, a venerable warrior with only a brief and single experience of active service. Sir Arthur kept his annoyance to himself and instead devoted his mind to questions of organization. At first everything seemed like the Indian wars all over again. Transport and supplies would be the all-important clues to success. The French armies were accustomed to live off the countries in which they fought, but in this case those countries were already near starvation point. There was need once more for bullock carts and for pack mules, for cordage and for canvas to protect supplies. With little help from headquarters in London, who had, among other things, quite forgotten to provide transport, Sir Arthur obtained the cattle that would be needed for fresh meat and somehow found waggons to carry stores and ammunition.

The Peninsular forces landed at Mondego Bay in the first week of August. A howling gale pounded the shore with a noise that could be heard ten miles out to sea, and a number of ship's boats were smashed to pieces in the boiling surf. Five days were to pass before Sir Arthur could review his assembled army on land. It was typical of him that his orders on how they, as Protestants, were to conduct themselves in a Catholic country, should include careful instructions to present arms when the Host was passing through the streets. They marched off with a burning sun over their heads and hot, shifting sand beneath their feet. The bullock-carts groaned dismally, the donkeys brayed, and soon the army was swinging into the direction of Lisbon.

After a brief dash at Obidos they came to Roliça, where the French had fallen back on a strongly defended table-land at the front of the village. It was a pretty spot with neat little houses and well-stocked vineyards. The country that lay about was dotted with olive groves and thickets, while beyond there towered ridge after ridge of a mountain chain. On the morning of the 17th the mists dissolved from the peaks to reveal a brilliant sun. Only the notes of bird song disturbed the quiet. Suddenly the boom of cannon broke out and reverberated in echoes around the hills. Sir Arthur had preferred an outflanking movement, but the rashness of one of his officers committed him to a frontal assault. Through the defiles and up the rock-strewn slopes toiled the English. Sparks flashed as bayonets crossed at their first encounter with the enemy, and gradually the French were squeezed back into the narrow mountain passes at the rear. Here, eventually, they were dislodged after hand-to-hand fighting alongside precipitous gorges where a slip of the foot could send a man hurtling down sheer rock-face. At four o'clock in the afternoon the last plume of smoke from the last fusillade drifted away and the sun shone clear again. The road to Lisbon lay wide open.

The victory at Roliça was important for several reasons. It demonstrated triumphantly to the rest of the world that Napoleon's men were not, as the legend tended to imply, unbeatable. The effect on the morale of the British was galvanic. They had proved themselves on their first meeting with the enemy, and now they looked forward with confidence to other encounters. Sir Arthur had shown himself as shrewd a commander in European warfare as he had in India. His men regarded him with admiration and respect. They knew that he concerned himself intimately with every stage of the battle and that he was as fully committed as they themselves were. With their own eyes they had seen him personally reconnoitring the enemy positions, explaining to each leader of a column exactly what his plans were, and doing it all with a calm cheerfulness that gave them added assurance. They knew, too, that whenever events took a bad turn, Sir Arthur was always at the place where danger threatened most, deploying his forces, as somebody put it, 'as a skilful dealer distributes his cards at a game of whist'. The men had rarely been able to identify themselves so completely with a leader. From Roliça onwards they trusted in him utterly.

A few days later, at Vimeiro, the British were on the defensive. A large force under Junot came out from Lisbon to attack. Junot was one of Napoleon's bravest generals and had won for himself the nickname of 'La Tempête' on account of his dashing exploits.

With a considerable flourish he threw his troops against the waiting redcoats. The French column charged forward, their nerves a little frayed by the silence with which the British greeted them. They went on like this until they were nearly eye to eye. And then, with appalling unexpectedness, round upon round of cannon split their ranks, a steady fusillade of musketry mowed them down, and bayonets closed in upon them. 'Now, Twentieth, now's the time!' shouted Sir Arthur, and his cavalry dashed victoriously upon the stricken brigades. Junot himself made a hair's breadth escape from capture. The British in the ranks grinned at each other and turned to look at their commander as he rode by, neat and close-shaven in his sombre frock-coat and cocked hat. The 'long-nosed b—', as they called him, had done it again.

By this time Wellesley's superior officers, Burrard and Dalrymple, had arrived from England and watched the last stages of the fight. 'Now's your time to advance, Sir Harry,' exclaimed Wellesley. 'The enemy are completely beaten, and we shall be in Lisbon in three days.' But Sir Harry, indecisive and jealous of the younger man's success, ordered the disappointed army to halt and not to pursue the fleeing enemy. Bewildered officers crowded round to ask Wellesley what they should do next. 'Shoot partridges', he snapped irritably. Just then a French emissary arrived bearing a white flag and suing for armistice. The bumbling Dalrymple conducted negotiations, and after six hours of argument produced an armistice agreement which, though he was too foolish to realize it, quite threw away the advantages that Wellesley's strategy had gained. Though Wellesley thoroughly deplored the agreement and had no hand whatever in drawing it up, he was ordered to sign it. He obeyed. He was sick of the way victory had been squandered, disgusted with the slights that had been put upon him, and he heartily wished he had never left Ireland.

The sky turned leaden and autumn rains began to drizzle on the British army around Lisbon. Burrard and Dalrymple continued their dreary bungling and committed yet another masterpiece of idiocy. This was known as the Convention of Cintra, an agreement laying down the terms by which the French were to evacuate Portugal. It was a confused document which, like the armistice, undid all the good work that had been done. On this occasion

Wellesley did not sign. Needless to say, the only positive result it had was to encourage Napoleon to act precisely as he had done before, and the exultant Emperor carried on with still more ambitious plans to dominate Portugal and Spain.

Wellesley landed at Plymouth on a grey October day. He did not expect a hero's welcome. His pessimism was well-founded. Public opinion raged furiously about the Convention of Cintra. Most unjustly, Wellesley was blamed equally with the others for having spoilt the fruits of victory. He went up to London and found everyone in a tumult of anger. 'Arrived here this day,' he reported to his brother, 'and I don't know whether I am to be hanged drawn and quartered; or roasted alive. However I shall not allow the Mob of London to deprive me of my temper or my spirits; or the satisfaction which I feel in the consciousness that I acted right.' The Whigs screamed for his blood and the newspapers covered him with shrill abuse. A statement from him would soon have cleared the air. He refused to make it. As a serving officer he argued it would be presumptuous of him to do so. That was the responsibility of the government, his employer. He did not even bother to point out that he had not signed the Convention. Excessive blame, like excessive praise, left him outwardly indifferent.

Such was the storm that in the end the government was forced to hold a court of enquiry. The findings gently reproved the leading culprits, 'Dowager' Dalrymple and 'Betty' Burrard, as Wellesley scathingly called them in private, and they faded away from public life. No-one, decided the enquiry, was to blame. Wellesley shrugged his shoulders. Too proud to use the weapons of his detractors, too honourable to attack former colleagues however bad their treatment of him, he was content with his own awareness that he was in the right. The wild fluctuations of mob opinion were fit only for his contempt. The affair had been a useful, if tiresome, lesson.

9. TOP: *The Battle of Vittoria, 21 July 1813.*   (By permission of the British Museum.)

10. BOTTOM: *The Battle of the Pyrenees, 28 July 1813.*   (By permission of the British Museum.)

# Peninsular:
# Second Phase

11. *Equestrian portrait of Wellington by Goya, 1812.* *(By permission of the Victoria and Albert Museum.)*

4

In the Spanish town of Corunna Sir John Moore lay dying. It was the 16 January, 1809. Moore, who was Burrard's successor as commander of the Peninsular army, had led his troops into Spain and struck towards Burgos, an important link in the French defences. His tactics were good and his planning was intelligent, but circumstances went against him. The decision to enter Spain was made too late. By the time Moore was on the march winter had set in. The roads were sloppy with mud, blizzards howled across the bare countryside, and mountain passes were choked with drifts. What was surprising about Moore's ill-fated campaign was not the fact that in the end he should have had to retreat, but that he should at the same time have managed to inflict several defeats on a large and powerful enemy. For Napoleon in person was directing the French troops. With his brother Joseph restored to the Spanish throne, he was determined once and for all to clear the Peninsular of the 'hateful presence' of the English. The astonishing speed with which he moved his huge forces across country in the abominable weather was largely achieved by the magic of his personality. He put himself at the head of the column and led them resolutely through sheeting hail and flurrying snow. Soldiers who had previously hesitated before precarious banks of snow were now fired by the Emperor's example and tramped forward with new energy.

In the early days of January Napoleon was forced to turn his attention elsewhere. Austria had decided to go against him, and the news was important enough to send him racing back to Paris to deal with this new threat. As events turned out, it was to mark a decisive point in his fortunes. From the moment the anxious courier handed the dispatch over to him, things began to go badly. Leaving one of his best generals to pursue Moore and the retreating British army, the Emperor ordered the Imperial Guard to cross the Pyrenees again and himself galloped at top speed to his headquarters in France. It was, of course, only over a period of several years that the tide of affairs could be seen to have turned to his disadvantage. At that precise moment things could not have looked blacker for Moore and his men as they ploughed laboriously back through the whirling snowstorms to the coast town of Corunna.

Here they rallied and took up position to defend their embarkation. The prelude to battle was a tremendous and ear-splitting explosion caused by the firing of a Spanish arsenal to prevent it passing into the hands of the enemy. Four thousand barrels of gunpowder were detonated in a blinding flash that sent a gigantic tower of smoke spiralling up in lazy, ever-broadening circles. By 15 January the fleet had arrived and the army began to embark, leaving the infantry, who were to take ship at nightfall, ready for the attack. Next day the French thrust boldly forward and were met by an equally determined defence. The struggle was grim, but at twilight the French were retreating in disorder. Had the light lasted a few more hours their defeat would have been disastrous.

Moore's satisfaction at this successful engagement was short-lived. A bullet struck him in the chest as he was directing the battle and he fell to the ground in mortal pain. The dying general was carried back to the citadel. 'Not a drum was heard, not a funeral note', on the chilly midnight air as his men laid the body in its hurriedly dug grave and read the burial service by torchlight. His death in the midst of victory was a poignant inspiration of the poem which commemorates the event –

> We carved not a line, we raised not a stone,
> But we left him alone with his glory,

run some of the best-known lines in English poetry.

The report of Sir John Moore's death caused a wave of emotion in England. He had been a chivalrous, honest man, a plain soldier with little taste for intrigue or politics. He quickly became, and has remained, a national hero. The government, though, had little time for romantic regret, since Spain and Portugal were rapidly sinking deeper under French domination. As usual, the Cabinet turned to Sir Arthur Wellesley, now back at his post as Irish Secretary but always ready to look at their problems for them. His advice was direct and simple. Portugal, he said, could be defended, even if Spain gave way completely to the French. The British army in Portugal should be built up and a commander sent out to take charge of it. The Cabinet fell in with his proposals. They gave him the Portuguese command into the bargain, and Lieutenant-General Wellesley, soon to be also Marshal-General of the Portuguese army, prepared himself for the familiar sight of Mondego Bay.

He did so with pleasurable excitement. The prospect of exchanging family life for service abroad was to be welcomed. A second son had been born the previous year, but even so the home in Harley Street remained a trying experience. Kitty was as clinging as ever. Her shortsightedness, too, was an embarrassment on social occasions, and her timidity handicapped a man who had to play the host at important public gatherings. She worried hopelessly over the household accounts yet was terrified of confessing the debts she was incurring, for she knew his horror of owing money. In the place of her flutterings and reproachful silences he could look forward to a campaigner's life again. The boring sessions of helping her to balance her budget were replaced by the more inviting task of organizing supplies for the new Portuguese contingent. His mind roved endlessly over sources of horse-shoes, nails, trenching tools, hammers, muskets and uniforms. He studied maps and visualized manoeuvres around the bleak sierras. The problems of Irish agriculture were forgotten as he eagerly perused the documents relating to Moore's ill-starred campaign and meditated fresh solutions. Parliament and the Irish Office knew him no more. Kitty and the family were packed off to Malvern, and while they settled obediently there Sir Arthur cantered down the Plymouth Road to take ship for his new command.

The *Surveillante*, English by nature though strangely French in name, weighed anchor just a few weeks before his fortieth birthday. She stood out from Portsmouth and almost immediately rocked into a violent gale in mid-Channel. The Captain began to think of making a desperate attempt to run ashore on the Isle of Wight, and a worried officer, screaming above the din of snapping ropes and mountainous waves, told his commander that they were doomed. 'In that case,' replied Sir Arthur coolly, 'I shall not take off my boots.' Despite a rough and tempestuous journey Sir Arthur's boots remained dry, and he arrived in Lisbon to a warm reception from the Portuguese. A week or so afterwards he assembled his army at Coimbra, and with this mixed force of English, Portuguese and Germans, he was ready to start operations.

His first objective was the town of Oporto. At the time this was occupied by Soult, a brilliant French marshal who had risen from the rank of corporal to general in seven short years. He had led the attack against Sir John Moore at Corunna, and now he lay at Oporto with a strong force of veteran troops. His position was an excellent one, for between him and the British rolled the dark waters of the river Douro. Sir Arthur came to its banks and halted before a deep, fast-flowing current at least three hundred yards wide. The bridges had been destroyed, fords were non-existent, and there was no sign of a boat for miles around. His eye fell upon a seminary at the other side. If that could be taken, by however small a force, then he would have gained the foothold that was so essential. But how was he to get his men over what seemed to be an impassable torrent?

One of his staff captains, a sharp-eyed soldier called Waters, happened to spot a skiff hidden among the tall reeds and stuck in the mud at the edge of the bank. Its owner, a Portuguese, had managed to evade Soult's patrols and was struggling to free his boat. Waters ran to help him. With the aid of peasants the skiff was eased into the current and snaked across to the opposite bank. Soon the little party returned leading a procession of several roomy barges they had discovered.

'By God! Waters has done it!' swore Sir Arthur delightedly. 'Let the men cross!'

Still unobserved by the enemy, twenty pieces of cannon were ferried over to the seminary. By the time the shrapnel was hurtling among the astonished French, it was too late for them to fight back successfully. The Portuguese inhabitants of Oporto, who detested the invader, rushed out to launch their own boats on the Douro and to help the British cross. Within a few hours Soult realized that he was fighting a losing battle. What was worse, he learned at the same time that Sir Arthur's colleague, General Beresford, had cut off his line of retreat higher up the Douro. With a last defiant flash of spirit, he refused to surrender and destroyed all his cannon and equipment so that nothing of value should fall into British hands. Then he turned abruptly and led the crushed remnants of his army through heavy rain over mountain tracks and arduous pathways until they collapsed, days later, a tattered and weary mob, in the first Spanish town they reached.

The operation was carried out with such brilliance and speed that on the night of May 12 Sir Arthur and his staff were able to enjoy the very dinner which had been prepared for Soult in his headquarters. It had taken only a fortnight to clear Soult out of Portugal, and less than a month passed before the country was entirely free of the unwanted invader. Perhaps Soult's biggest mistake – and it was one that his compatriots often made – was to under-estimate his opponent. This was something Sir Arthur himself never did. Despite his sweeping defeat of the French marshal, he had respect for him and commented that '. . . though his plans seemed always to be admirable, he never knew when to strike'.

Yet victory, as Sir Arthur well knew, could bring as many problems as defeat. 'I have long been of opinion, that a British army could bear neither success nor failure . . .' he wrote acidly when reports of indiscipline and wholesale plundering came in after Oporto. Once again he had to act ruthlessly to curb men who were running wild and raiding the countryside. If the activities of his own troops were bad enough, he was to find when he marched into Spain that those of his new allies were still more tiresome.

The Spanish army that was to assist him against the French aroused his worst fears. They were unwilling and uncooperative. He concluded that '. . . to manoeuvre with such a rabble under fire, is impossible. I am afraid we shall find them an encumbrance rather than otherwise.' The same might have been said of their nominal commander, a venerable gentleman with the splendid name of El Capitan-General Don Gregorio de la Cuesta. So ancient was he that he had to be supported in his saddle by a page at either side of his horse. He rarely kept an appointment, usually dropped off to sleep at the crucial moment, and had never won a battle in the whole of his life. And in addition to all the other hindrances facing Sir Arthur, support from England in the shape of money and supplies began to fall away.

The Spanish campaign, therefore, started under bad auspices. Sir Arthur commanded a force of some forty thousand troops together with the disorganized and unreliable Spanish army. Against him were arrayed two hundred and fifty thousand French soldiers under Napoleon's finest generals, each of them placed at strategic points and all with excellent lines of communication. On a hot afternoon in July Sir Arthur halted his advance into central Spain near the city of Talavera. A strong French contingent was stationed nearby under General Victor, a commander who, like so many of Napoleon's marshals, had begun in the ranks. He enlisted as a drummer and had quickly been rewarded for his excellent leadership. While Sir Arthur paused cautiously to reconnoitre the dusty plain and the arid hillocks that shimmered in the heat-haze before the French positions, the Spanish general Cuesta suddenly exploded into action. Ignoring his English friend's commonsense advice, the irresponsible old warrior hared off with his men in a foolhardy attempt to capture Madrid. A few days later he was back, thoroughly discomforted and smartly out-manoeuvred by Victor.

At three o'clock in the afternoon of July 27 the French came forward to attack. Almost immediately the Spanish troops broke ranks and vanished in the dust. 'They are really children in the art of war,' said the exasperated Sir Arthur, 'and I cannot say that they do anything as it ought to be done, with the exception of running away and assembling in a state of nature.' He was left alone with his men to fight a tense engagement at the end of which the French were turned back. As darkness fell, neither side had won or lost a single inch of ground, and two thousand soldiers lay dead.

At five in the morning fighting began again. Four hours later, as if by some unspoken agreement, the guns fell silent and men from both armies quenched their thirst in a small stream that ran through the battlefield. They chatted together and exchanged flasks in the burning heat. Then the drums beat to arms, the men remembered that they were soldiers, and the opposing armies formed up again. That afternoon forty thousand Frenchmen thundered in a great wave along the whole of the British line. At one point they would have broken through had it not been for the presence of Sir Arthur, who, always at the spot where he knew trouble might be expected, was able to direct a successful counter-attack. A spent bullet had bruised him on the chest, but he ignored it, galloping up and down the lines through the shafts of hot sunlight that pierced the swirling smoke, his face impassive, his eyes noting every significant detail. The slaughter was immense. Several hundred dragoons, ordered to charge over treacherous ground at the massed French infantry, thudded forward and flew one after another into a concealed ravine which quickly piled up with heaps of dying men and horses. Out on the plain, fallen leaves, parched to the consistency of tinder, were ignited by blazing cartridge papers, and in the hot weather a wall of flame leapt up and engulfed the wounded men who lay helpless on the ground.

The battle swayed fiercely on all through the day and into the damp cold night. At dawn the weary British re-grouped and stood by for the next assult. It never came. Victor and his forty thousand men had given up and marched away. The British had won a victory – true, a muddled, bloody and hideously confused one, but nevertheless a victory. Sir Arthur took stock. His army was exhausted and starving. More and stronger French forces lurked waiting for him along the winding Spanish roads. He wanted no more to do with the incompetent allies who had been thrust upon him, and he longed to be free of their obstinacy and their obstruction. 'I have fished in many troubled waters, but Spanish troubled waters I will never fish in again', he observed as he wheeled round his army and led them back towards the Portuguese frontier.

'Never was there such a Murderous Battle!!' Sir Arthur told

his brother. Talavera was hailed with enthusiasm by his country-men. At last, it seemed, Britain had a general who knew how to succeed on land as Nelson had at sea. Coaches decked with laurel and flowers carried the news to cheering crowds the length and breadth of the land. A dispatch arrived at Badajoz, near the Portuguese frontier where the army was in camp, telling Sir Arthur that he was now a peer. The choice of a title was a little difficult, and since he had more important things to think about he left the matter to one of his brothers. Eventually a solution was found. A remote ancestor, it seemed, had once owned land near the village of Wellington in Somerset. Sir Arthur, quite un-impressed and a shade amused by all the fuss, found himself con-verted into Baron Douro of Wellesley and Viscount Wellington of Talavera, with a yearly income of two thousand pounds for three years voted to him by a grateful House of Commons.

These new honours, to which were added other resounding titles bestowed upon him by Spain and Portugal, made little difference to the life of Wellington, as he was henceforward to be known. As the autumn days drew in at Badajoz he continued the simple, hard-working routine he had always followed. He was up early in the morning to write letters and despatches before break-fast. The meal was followed by discussions with heads of staff about the day's work, and then he went on with his correspondence until two. In the afternoon he would usually ride out on a tour of in-spection, or perhaps vary the procedure with some 'pretty good sport' shooting deer around Badajoz. At six o'clock he had company in to dinner, and round about nine he retired to his own room and continued with his correspondence until midnight, for he was an astonishingly prolific and conscientious letter writer. Yet however grave his responsibilities may have been at any given time, he was always able, like many other famous leaders, to empty his mind of worry and fall asleep whenever and wherever he wished.

While the British and their commander lay at Badajoz gathering their forces, training and equipping themselves, and preparing for their next combat, the Spanish army dissipated its strength in ill-advised engagements with the French. An early victory was quickly followed by a string of heavy defeats, and by the end of the year the impulsive campaign had resulted in the southern part of the country being exposed to the enemy. In the spring of 1810 the French were everywhere on the move. They were hampered, though, by a thoughtful move Wellington had instituted earlier on. This was his order for a 'scorched earth' policy to be carried out in Portugal. The French army, he knew, carried very little food with them and made a practice of living off the countries they passed through. Overcoming the understandable reluctance of the Portuguese, he persuaded them to destroy, systematically, all the crops in the areas where the French were expected, and all the mills, and also to remove all the cattle and wine that were likely to be found in the path of the oncoming invaders. Then he secured Lisbon with a thick and formidable line of defences at Torres Vedras and chose a position just over the Portuguese frontier. It was a long time before the enemy came, and his nerves tautened as spring slipped by into summer. He thought the trial of strength would come at Busaco, and there he plotted the terrain and laid out his forces.

At last, in July, fifty-seven thousand French crossed the frontier under Masséna, a marshal for whom Wellington, in the course of the battles they fought against each other, was to learn to have a healthy respect. He was, said Wellington, '. . . by far the ablest of Bonaparte's marshals that I had anything to do with. . . . His great blunder was in facing me as long as he did.' On this occasion, indeed, Masséna's progress was slow, if not leisurely. Before entering Portugal he had taken Ciudad Rodrigo, a fortress that meant more to the Spanish than to Wellington, who was not very concerned about its loss. Far more worrying was the fall of Almeida, a town just inside the Portuguese frontier. By a rare chance a shell set light to the powder magazine. The explosion wrecked nearly every building in the place, and Almeida surrendered without a battle. This bad news coming at such an early stage alarmed the authorities in England, and they proposed to send out some more senior officers from the same stable as the unlamented Dalrymple and Burrard. 'I only hope,' declared the harassed Wellington, 'that when the enemy reads the list of their names he trembles as I do.'

As Masséna and his army lumbered on from Almeida, they found with increasing dismay that Wellington's 'scorched earth' plans had been almost wholly successful. Instead of the plump cattle and stores of corn they relied upon for essential supplies, they came across deserted barns and empty granaries. By the time Wellington first caught the distant glitter of their bayonets and the clouds of dust raised by the tramping battalions, Masséna's forces were already unsettled by hunger and by the swooping attacks of guerillas on the way. Towards the end of September they filtered through the hills and around the heathery slopes in front of Busaco. In the thick fogs of dawn on September 26, the French battled up in the direction of Wellington's shrewdly chosen defensive position on a high ridge. They lunged heavily through the coiling mists to be met with a spirited repulse. British morale was high, for Wellington's presence and manner, as an eye-witness remarked, 'gave that confidence to his companions which had a magical effect'. Even when the French succeeded in piercing the defences and momentarily gaining the peak of the ridge, Wellington's intuition brought him speedily to the rescue with orders that were 'short, quick, clear and to the purpose'.

Masséna soon realized the futility of continuing an action that had already cost him little short of five thousand men, and he withdrew his troops. Wellington now followed his pre-arranged plan and moved back to the fortifications which he had spent so many careful months in building at Torres Vedras near Lisbon. Masséna followed on under heavy rain, hoping for a moment that Wellington planned to evacuate by sea. When, however, he saw through his telescope the formidable lines of Torres Vedras, he could scarcely believe his eyes. The chain of mountains bristled with artillery and impregnable outposts. Behind them, though Masséna did not as yet know this, stood a second line of thickly fortified redoubts and emplacements. Yet another and third line of fieldworks between the river Tagus and the hills of Cintra completed the triply strong defensive arrangements.

Mid-way through October Wellington looked down on Masséna's army encamped before Torres Vedras and mused: 'Damned tempting, damned tempting. . . . I could lick those fellows any day, but it would cost me ten thousand men, and as this is the last army England has, we must take care of it.' Regretfully, he decided that the sure 'game' was to wait for Masséna to attack – or to starve. And the two armies stared tensely at each other across the tremendous tangle of fortifications, while the drifting autumn rains began to swell the rivers and flood the countryside.

# The Way to Paris

12. *The Battle of Salamanca, 1812.* *(By permission of the British Museum.)*

5

Under the watery November skies Wellington continued building more defence works, hoping that the French would fall into the trap of launching an attack. 'Masséna is an old fox and as cautious as I am,' he said. 'He risks nothing.' So 'The Peer', as his men now nicknamed him half mockingly, half respectfully, went on with his waiting game. Money was short – it always was – and he complained to the government that he did not get one-sixth of what was needed to pay for supplies. He solved the matter by establishing his own currency and buying from American ships the corn with which he saved his army and the people of Lisbon from starvation. Politicians in England had little idea of the practical difficulties he faced. Worse still, they thought that he had been driven into a tight corner by Masséna and was on the verge of defeat, whereas, of course, the situation was completely the reverse. Swallowing his annoyance with the unintelligent gentlemen at home, Wellington pressed his demand for one hundred thousand pairs of shoes. It might, he reminded them, be necessary to march forward soon. . . .

By the middle of November Masséna s army was starving and in low spirits. Frustrated in their attempts to forage an exhausted countryside and perpetually annoyed by partisan fighters, they marched away on a dark foggy night. Like Sir John Moore, Wellington chose to make for Burgos as his ultimate objective. But this time there would be ample preparation. First of all he would set his sights at Badajoz and Ciudad Rodrigo. In the meantime, he followed warily at the rear of the French. Only when he entered Santarem early in March 1811, was he fully convinced that Masséna was genuinely retreating. Then, in quick succession at Pombal, Redinha, and Foz D'Aronce, he scored a series of quick victories which hastened the stumbling withdrawal of Masséna and his forces.

Spring showers chilled the barefooted French soldiers as they struggled along the roads and threw away their equipment to ease their tired shoulders. Desperate for food, they murdered and raped in the villages that lay on their path. They poisoned the water by throwing the dead bodies of their victims into wells, and behind them they left a trail of slaughter and destruction. In the dank grey fog of Sabugal Masséna fought a last engagement, and then crossed the border to make for Salamanca. The French were out of Portugal for good, yet they still menaced the frontier with their possession of the Portuguese border town of Almeida and the Spanish fortress of Badajoz, over a hundred and thirty miles away. Riding so hard that two horses died under him, Wellington covered the distance in three days, weighing up the situation at Badajoz and drafting siege orders before dashing north again to face Masséna, who had re-assembled with fresh troops. The French marshal, counting on the heavy rains to hold up Wellington, was hastening to relieve Almeida. The English intercepted him on the upland of Fuentes de Oñoro, where for two days the French in their tall plumed hats grappled on the slopes with their opponents in the red coats. The British infantry formed into squares and held firm under repeated cavalry charges, while up and down the village streets Highlanders bitterly contested every inch of ground to the Emperor's grenadiers. By May 8 the French had left the wooded crags of Fuentes de Oñoro and were in retreat. Two days afterwards Masséna was relieved of his command.

Soon Almeida fell to the English, although Masséna's garrison, profiting from an oversight, contrived to escape. Wellington's anger at his commanders' lack of generalship was so fearsome that one of them shot himself. An equally empty victory was to follow at Albuera, where Beresford stuck it out in a dogged battle with Soult and finally routed him. Only fifteen hundred British infantry remained out of the six thousand who had gone into the fight, and these were losses that could ill be afforded. Another such battle, Wellington observed, would ruin them. He decided, nonetheless, to carry out the next stage of his plan and to recapture Badajoz which lay nearby. This he attempted without much optimism, for he lacked both equipment and engineers. His battering-train was badly in need of repair, and some of the guns he used were more than two centuries old. Time, that most valuable commodity, was not on his side either, and before June was out he sensibly withdrew and turned his attention to Ciudad Rodrigo. There again he was foiled. The French commander Marmont had now taken over from the disgraced Masséna. The son of an army officer and himself a professional soldier, Marmont had figured among Napoleon's later promotions, and he took up his command with all the fresh enthusiasm of a newcomer. Unknown to Wellington, he had revictualled Ciudad Rodrigo with enough supplies to last a good eight months. The British army moved over the exposed land around the town and fought a stiff skirmish on the bare heights of El Bodon. So close was the battle that Wellington himself had to fight with his drawn sword. The absence of one of his generals at a crucial moment caused him intense displeasure, and the following day he made sure the errant officer was aware of it.

'I am glad to see you safe, General Craufurd,' he observed chillingly.

'I was never in danger,' came the airy response.

'Oh! I was,' said Wellington briefly.

'He's damned crusty this morning,' said Craufurd to himself.

The crustiness was not to be wondered at. Wellington had by now spent almost three years under continuous battle conditions. He had to contend not only with an enemy who invariably outnumbered him in men and equipment, but also with an army which he must constantly train and invigorate. Another thorn in his side was the untrustworthy allies whose presence was more of a handicap than anything else. All the work had to be done with but timid, cheeseparing assistance from a British government which did not always succeed in appreciating the difficulties he laboured under. And all the time the Whig opposition was attacking him in Parliament with such virulence, indeed slander, that the French hoped they would soon succeed the Tories. A Whig government, reasoned Napoleon, would be much more favourable to him. It is not too much to say that, but for Wellington, the Peninsular campaign would quickly have ended in defeat. Everything depended upon one man, and the responsibility he carried was tremendous. Often in the saddle from morning to night, he bore intense physical and mental strain with a constitution that more than justified his later sobriquet of the 'Iron Duke'. His self-control in the teeth of events that would have wrecked any other man's confidence made his occasional outbursts all the more terrible. Usually a laconic rebuke or an ironical shaft was the most he allowed himself. He had, said a close acquaintance, 'the best nerves of anyone I ever met with'.

During the autumn of 1811 he laid his plans for the capture of Ciudad Rodrigo. His orders contrast amusingly with those of Napoleon, who filled his proclamations with stirring calls to glory. Instead of issuing grandiloquent appeals to martial pride, Wellington concentrated on nails for horse-shoes and adequate supplies of army biscuit. He came to work in a drab grey frock-coat that the French generals, resplendent in their decorations and gold lace, would have despised. His only concession to sartorial display was the blue and black uniform of the Salisbury Hunt which he donned to ride to hounds across the plains of Portugal. He was so totally immersed in his work that he could not help feeling surprised when officers applied for leave. One of his staff was grudgingly allowed forty-eight hours in Lisbon with the comment that such a period was 'as long as any reasonable man can wish to stay in bed with the same woman'. From time to time his raucous laugh – 'very loud and long, like the whoop of the whooping cough often repeated' – would be heard in the mess. Most of the time, though, he rarely unbent, and his lonely days were fully occupied with organizing the siege train and the supplies that would be needed to invest Ciudad Rodrigo.

On 7 January he moved through snow and frost to assault the town. It was a strangely still and beautiful day. The smoke of twenty-seven roaring guns soon cloaked the lower ramparts in a dense veil. Out of it rose the towers and roofs above, like something in a fairy tale. Gradually the redoubts crumbled under incessant pounding. Trenches were opened, parallels traced, scarps broached, and within ten days or so Wellington was being presented with the large and heavy key to the fortress of Ciudad Rodrigo.* Without pausing to celebrate the new honour of an earldom, nor his promotion as Duque de Ciudad Rodrigo, he rushed on as fast as he could to his next objective at Badajoz. For speed now was essential, and by securing Badajoz he would have closed Portugal for ever to the French. A system of flying bridges enabled him to get his troops over the river Guadiana and within striking distance of the town. There he found that the defenders had laid a complicated network of galleries and trenches with the purpose of mining his batteries. The whole place was so well fortified that it cost him a desperate effort to take it.

Wellington knew only too well the penalty of failure, and again and again his infantry were ordered to charge into breaches secured by massive iron chains bristling with bayonets and naked swords. The main assault took place on the night of 6 April. Wellington surveyed the battle from a height lit by blue lights, rockets, flaming shells and blazing grapeshot. By the gleam of a flickering torch somebody came with a premature report of failure. A bystander noted the effect on Wellington. 'The jaw had fallen, the face was of unusual length, while the torchlight gave his countenance a lurid aspect; but still the expression of the face was firm.' Just then news arrived that the citadel was breached. After two hours of monstrous slaughter the castle fell, discipline vanished in the heady excitement of victory, and for three days and nights Wellington's army rioted uncontrollably in debauch, regardless of the gallows their angry commander erected for the culprits. With their teeth they wrenched women's rings from their fingers, and they desecrated churches with every kind of outrage and murder. It is not surprising that Wellington had little regard for

* The key is preserved at Apsley House.

'the scum of the earth' who marched under his command. But when he saw the unusually long list of the dead, he broke down for once and wept.

Now that Ciudad Rodrigo and Badajoz were in British hands, the logical next step was to invade Spain. For the time being the heavy seasonal rains kept both armies shut up in their camps. Swollen rivers and swampy plains gave them an excellent reason for lying low, and the opportunity for a rest was eagerly seized. As usual, Wellington's problems were not exclusively military. There was, for example, the ever-present question of finance. That spring the troops had not been paid for five months, the muleteers had not received any money since June of the previous year, and Wellington's own staff were several months in arrears. In April he wrote to the Prime Minister that he owed 'not less than five million dollars'. Since the Spanish dollar was worth six shillings in the money of the time, the size of the debt in modern currency can be appreciated. Wellington's appeal soon brought one hundred thousand pounds in gold from England, and in the meantime he was able to think over his next move.

Half-way through June 1812, Wellington's mind was made up and he darted quickly for Salamanca, where Marmont was established. The army moved across wooded countryside whose midsummer green under a clear blue sky clashed oddly with the snowy peaks of the Sierra de Gata. A few days later Wellington led his troops into Salamanca and was mobbed by the cheering towns-people who thronged excitedly around him, and, in their enthusi-asm, nearly tore the quiet, unmoving figure off his horse. The real work was to come two days afterwards when he launched his attack against some strongly defended forts outside the town to which Marmont had retired. With only a few eighteen-pounders and twenty-four-pounder iron howitzers, the British managed after a tough struggle to clear out Marmont by the end of the month.

Marmont continued his retreat well into July. By that time, anxious to break the deadlock and eager for revenge, he was manoeuvring to cut off Wellington's line of retreat and recapture Salamanca. In attempting to do this he committed the tactical error of moving unawares right across the British army's front. Wellington, 'stumping about and munching' a piece of cold chicken in a nearby farmyard, clapped his telescope to his eye and saw what was going on. 'By God,' he shouted, 'that will do!' He flung the chicken bone over his shoulder and rushed to mount his horse Copenhagen. A closer look convinced him that Marmont was playing right into his hands, and he galloped headlong from position to position, issuing his orders in person and looking pale with excitement. He joined in the infantry advance and then gave orders for the heavy cavalry to charge, remarking to their commander as they did so: 'By God, Cotton, I never saw anything so beautiful in my life; the day is *yours*'. It was. Within forty minutes, it was later reckoned, forty thousand Frenchmen were crushingly defeated. Marmont lost over fourteen thousand troops and was himself so badly wounded that he had to be carried off the field. The battle of Salamanca, conceded one of the French generals a few days later, '. . . raises Lord Wellington almost to the level of Marlborough . . . he has shown himself a great and able master of manoeuvres. . . .'

Everywhere, now, the French were scattered and in retreat. While Joseph, Napoleon's brother and king of Spain, fled with a large force to the safety of distant Valencia, Wellington made a hero's entry into Madrid. Bells pealed exultantly, windows and balconies were crammed with cheering spectators as the conqueror rode by, and in the street crowds swirled noisily about offering wine, flowers, tobacco and laurel to the marching troops. Wellington picked his way impassively amongst the waving coloured shawls and kept his grave demeanour even when black-eyed señoras rained kisses both upon him and upon his horse. The news of Salamanca brought quite as much rejoicing in England, and the King advanced Wellington another step in the Peerage by creating him a Marquess. 'What the devil is the use of making me a Marquess?' enquired the recipient of the new honour with cheerful irreverence. Yet he was not entirely indifferent to fame. One of his favourite relaxations in Madrid was to listen with obvious pleasure to songs in which a local musician celebrated his military deeds in the most florid of terms. Much more to the point was the sum of one hundred thousand pounds which Parliament had voted him in gratitude for the victory.

Salamanca has often been described as Wellington's 'masterpiece'. It assuredly ranks next after Waterloo. Nevertheless, the story was by no means over. Although the French were also suffering heavy reverses elsewhere – it was 1812 and the disastrous retreat from Moscow was soon to take place – they still had some two hundred thousand men in Spain. The well-nigh 'perfect' victory of Salamanca was succeeded by the failure to take Burgos. Pausing on the way from Madrid to capture the town of Valladolid, Wellington came upon Burgos early in autumn. But the rains had set in again and flooded his trenches, the enemy was massing in great numbers, and he had little ammunition or equipment. 'I played a game which might succeed (the only one which could succeed), and pushed it to the last . . .' he admitted ruefully, and drew off his army to find shelter in friendly Portugal. The necessary retreat that followed, he confessed, was 'the worst scrape that he ever was in'. The breakdown in transport and supplies that hampered him at Burgos continued to dog him as the army wended its slow way back beyond the river Douro. Discipline slacked off and starving men went plundering for food. Even Wellington's steady nerve gave way, and in a rage of exasperation caused partly by his failure to take Burgos, partly by fatigue, he issued a memorandum which bitterly reproached both officers and men. It was some time before they really forgave him this outburst.

At Freneda the army went into winter quarters. Battle-weary men forgot the miseries of the past few weeks and organized dances and amateur theatricals. The grey days rolled somnolently by and the monotony was varied with good-natured horseplay. The English Commander was described as 'in high spirits and great humour with everyone'. A recent attack of lumbago subsided enough to let him ride to hounds again, and the hills of Portugal resounded to English halloos. 'Lord Wellington looks forward very coolly to another winter next season,' it was remarked. 'He said yesterday he should have twenty-five couples of fox-hounds next season.' He also had the pleasant duty of sorting out all the honours that were pouring in upon him. The Spaniards had named him Generalissimo of the Spanish Armies. The Portuguese, not to be outdone by their neighbours, had made him Marquez de Torres Vedras and Duque da Vittoria. The trappings of Knight Grand Cross of the Tower and Sword reposed in his wardrobe, along with the diamond-encrusted Order of the Golden Fleece. Compared with all this, the Colonelcy of the Royal Regiment of the

Horse Guards and the Order of the Garter seemed modest indeed.*

The winter months in Portugal were a period of shattering events in other parts of the world. Napoleon's great Russian adventure crumbled into failure, and by December the Emperor himself was admitting defeat and the destruction of his finest army in the snowy reaches around Moscow. He had many other worries apart from Spain. Indeed, he started withdrawing some of his best troops for urgent service elsewhere, and the unfortunate king Joseph saw his army shrinking still more rapidly. The result was that in the early spring of 1813 the French forces were scattered unevenly over large areas of Spain. Wellington, on the other hand, had been extremely active all this time. While the French dithered uncertainly, he had been organizing guerilla attacks throughout the country to distract and harry them. He took advantage of the winter pause to consolidate good relations with the Spanish and Portuguese authorities. By the end of May, with valuable re-inforcements to swell his army, he knew that the hour had come to strike once and for all. Wisely refraining from crossing the Douro at a point where the enemy was likely to be massed in force, he slipped over the river in a basket on a cable, lower down its course, while another wing of his army marched on to Toro. As he rode over the Portuguese frontier he turned his horse and, rising in his stirrups with uncharacteristic flamboyance, he waved his hat and exclaimed: 'Farewell, Portugal! I shall never see you again.'

A few days later the two wings of the army were re-united at Toro as planned, the unexpected move having disconcerted the French and upset their scheme to intercept at Salamanca. Joseph and his army fell back in dismay and confusion. They were closely followed by Wellington and his men, who, as they passed through each town on the route, were greeted with cheers, showers of rose petals and tinkling tambourines. 'This singing psalms to me wastes time,' snapped Wellington testily, as he wrested with the un-romantic problems of biscuit and flour supplies. Burgos fell with little difficulty after a neat outflanking movement, and soon the British were launched on a march through the Cantabrian

---

* The enamelled badge of the Order, set with jewels, is at Apsley House. It was worn by Sir Winston Churchill at the coronation of Queen Elizabeth II in 1953.

Mountains that was to become famous. The men toiled through dry ravines and hauled cannon over wild and rugged chasms. It was the most difficult country they had ever tackled, but five days of lowering guns on ropes down rocky precipices, of clambering up narrow goatpaths, and of struggling across foaming torrents, ended triumphantly when they suddenly burst through and established themselves on the left bank of the river Ebro. The French, meanwhile, deeming the mountains impassable, saw no sign of their enemy and lived in a sense of false security. 'Is Lord Wellington asleep?' they asked in baffled tones.

The answer to the question came in the early dawn mist of June 21. Wellington swooped meteorically near the town of Vitoria and encircled the French, cutting them off from the road to Bayonne. 'Come on, ye rascals! Come on, ye fighting villains!' shouted the exuberant General Picton as he sent his men on a breathless charge that knocked the French out of several important positions. All day long Wellington never left his saddle and he seemed to be personally directing 'every movement of every corps in his army'. By late afternoon, from his position on a hillock, he could look down into the valley and see the French army breaking up everywhere under the repeated blows of British horse artillery, hussars and infantry. Joseph and his staff fled for their lives, relinquishing all their artillery, vast quantities of supplies, and a huge baggage train of plunder worth considerably more than a million pounds. Gold, jewels, silks, plate, and great chests of money lay scattered waiting to be looted. Joseph's own carriage, hurriedly deserted by its owner, was found to contain over a hundred and fifty valuable old paintings taken from the Spanish Royal collection.* Another curiosity was the baton of the French Marshal Jourdan. With certain adaptations, this served as the model for the baton, the first English one of its kind, that Wellington himself was to receive when the government promoted him to Field Marshal after Vitoria.

Now only the Pyrenees stood between the British army and the land of France. The two strong points that made Wellington think carefully before planning to invade were the fortress of San Sebastian and Pamplona, which lay on either side of the steep

* Wellington later offered to return them to the King of Spain. The King told him to keep them, and many of them can be seen at Apsley House.

ridges and gloomy valleys of the Pyrenees. Towards the end of July the siege of San Sebastian was begun. Meanwhile, a diversion at Sorauren, where the British commander, scribbling orders on the parapet of a bridge, narrowly escaped capture by French dragoons who came pounding up the street, foiled the enemy's attempt to re-enter Spain by way of Roncesvalles. Wellington's quick thinking and a dramatic change of plan saved the day. His men were in excellent form, and, as he remarked, 'they will do for me what perhaps no-one else can make them do'. His neat, grey-clad figure, silhouetted on horseback against the sky, was first glimpsed by Portuguese soldiers in the ranks. 'Douro! Douro!' they cheered enthusiastically. Then the British redcoats took up the cheer for 'old Nosey' and chuckled among themselves: "Ere's Atty, 'ere's that long nosed b—r that licks the French!'

It was Soult who led the French thrust at Roncesvalles – a warier, more cautious Soult than the marshal who first confronted Wellington outside Oporto four years ago. Yet once again he had attacked 'in the old style' and was beaten off. After a battle in which he suffered thirteen thousand casualties, he broke away and made one last effort to raise the siege of San Sebastian. He failed. The garrison capitulated to Wellington a few weeks later, and soon afterwards, starved out by a remorseless blockade, Pamplona opened its gates to the British army. 'I could have done *anything* with that army,' Wellington used to say in later years. 'It was in such splendid order.' And now, confident of victory, it stood poised to invade Napoleon's own country.

November came, and with it driving rain that hammered the roads and paths into a sea of mud. During a lull in the seemingly endless storms and gales, Wellington and his army carved through Soult's defence-works at the battle of the Nivelle. A few weeks later, after scrambling knee-deep in mud, they pushed Soult back beyond the River Nive and were established in French territory. There was a short lull after some skirmishing near Biarritz, and Wellington donned once more the buckskin breeches and black cap of the Salisbury Hunt to chase French foxes. He was relaxed and cheerful. Over the past years of campaigning the army had gradually been welded into an efficient fighting force. His staff, although he still insisted on overseeing every detail for himself and on trusting his own intuition to guess what the enemy was doing 'on the other side of the hill', had learned to appreciate the way his mind worked and to find the best way of carrying out his orders. In the Mess he was approachable and informal, his quick mind catching at ideas thrown out in conversation as he talked with his officers and scrutinized their expressions with his clear blue eyes. Hitherto quite indifferent to food, he now employed no less than three cooks, and winter quarters at Saint-Jean-de-Luz were improved with some excellent dinners at which guests were struck by the quality of the mutton and the wines that accompanied it.

In February of the following year Wellington pushed deeper into France. The river Adour was bridged with planking and tackle near Bayonne, and at Orthez that month Soult was thrown back further still in the stinging snowy winds that announced a blustery spring. On 12 March the British army entered Bordeaux led by their commander wearing a white cloak as if in deference to the unseasonable weather. Within a month they were at the gates of Toulouse, where Soult made a last desperate stand before vanishing with his beaten army into the darkness of the night. The Peninsular War was over.

Next day Wellington cantered into the city among loud cheers from the inhabitants, who now foreswore Napoleon and called for the restoration of Louis XVIII. Early that evening a rider galloped up with tremendous news. Napoleon had abdicated at Fontainebleau. 'How abdicated?' said Wellington. 'Ay, 'tis time indeed, you don't say so, upon my honour! Hurrah!' And his astonished companions saw the usually reticent 'Peer' spin gaily about snapping his fingers, his coat-tails flying in the wind. He went to on a grand ball at the Prefecture where the guests laughed, wept and shook hands for sheer excitement. A volatile Spanish general proposed a toast to 'The Liberator of Europe'. A tear gleamed momentarily in Wellington's eye. He rose, 'bowed, confused, and immediately called for coffee'.

# Waterloo

*LONDON, THURSDAY, JUNE 22, 1815.*

## OFFICIAL BULLETIN.

" DOWNING-STREET, JUNE 22, 1815.

" The Duke of WELLINGTON's Dispatch, dated Waterloo, the 19th of June, states, that on the preceding day BUONAPARTE attacked, with his whole force, the British line, supported by a corps of Prussians : which attack, after a long and sanguinary conflict, terminated in the complete Overthrow of the Enemy's Army, with the loss of ONE HUNDRED and FIFTY PIECES of CANNON and TWO EAGLES. During the night, the Prussians under Marshal BLUCHER, who joined in the pursuit of the enemy, captured SIXTY GUNS, and a large part of BUONAPARTE's BAGGAGE. The Allied Armies continued to pursue the enemy. Two French Generals were taken."

Such is the great and glorious result of those masterly movements by which the Hero of Britain met and frustrated the audacious attempt of the Rebel Chief. Glory to WELLINGTON, to our gallant Soldiers, and to our brave Allies ! BUONAPARTE's reputation has been wrecked, and his last grand stake has been

another of our columns. It contains an ac habitants of the Fauxbourgs St. Antoir ceau, and a Declaration in the name ORLEANS. Both these documents a ably drawn up. The one successfull ferocious doctrines of the Jacobins, more insidious views of those who ver their criminality with the resp to a brave and honourable Member of Bourbon. Whether his Serene authorised this avowal of his sentim not; but it is one, which appears genial with that fair and manly conduc alway observed. The Duke of ORLEA any time given the least countenance to the jects, which, under the specious pretence to himself, would as completely break ciple of legal succession, as if a BUONAP BESPIERRE were the object of election. once violated, the faction assumin right of choosing any given Sovereig morrow, with equal authority, assume cashiering him. Nothing would be secure. Neither King, nor Dynas of Government, would be certain twelvemonth ; the intolerable perpetu would necessitate the ultimate submis ism ; and none would be more miserat than those unfortunate personages {

13. *The Times announcement of the Battle of Waterloo.*

# 6

While Napoleon sailed off in exile to take up his derisory post as 'Emperor' of the tiny island of Elba, Wellington sat with the monarchs of Europe and the Czar of Russia to watch the Allied Armies on their victory parade through Paris. Then he saw England again for the first time in more than five years. His journey from Dover to London was a triumphant progress, and at Westminster Bridge the crowds unhorsed his carriage and pulled it cheering through the streets. A series of brilliant festivities was staged at which he was the guest of honour. Fêted by royalty, mobbed by crowds whenever he appeared in public, he could be forgiven for enjoying the favours that were showered upon him after the faint-hearted support and even hostility that had been his lot for several years. He did not lose his sense of proportion, and the most extravagant praises failed to dent his dignity. In the postscript of a letter to his brother, he mentioned casually: 'I believe I forgot to tell you I was made a Duke'. And as a further sign of gratitude, the nation voted its greatest soldier since Marlborough a gift of four hundred thousand pounds.

The name of Wellington was everywhere on people's lips. The famous 'Wellington boots' were named after an invention of his. There were Wellington hats, Wellington coats and Wellington trousers. A type of apple was christened in his honour, and so was a giant species of tree. Then and throughout the years to come, innumerable streets and public places were given the name of Wellington – there are well over twenty streets so named in London alone – not to mention the towns, buildings, warships and aircraft which commemorate the unforgettable impression the Duke made upon his countrymen. The fame and popularity he enjoyed as the saviour of Europe have only been approached in later years, though even then not equalled, by the reputation of Winston Churchill.

For the first time in a long and anxious period the world was at peace. There were no more battles for the Duke to fight. But idleness was not in his nature, and he soon returned to France as British Ambassador. It may have seemed odd to appoint as Ambassador to a country the very man who had only just conquered it. Yet the government's decision was a sound one. They had always claimed to be fighting Napoleon and not the nation of France. Moreover, the Duke was not only a soldier but also, now, a figure of international prestige, as well as being a brilliant administrator. So back he went to Paris, where he was joined by his wife Kitty and the family. Kitty was, perhaps, more scared of him and his new-found fame than ever. She knew that he had only married her since he believed she had deliberately kept herself free for him while he was in India. When he discovered, much too late, that she had in fact had another suitor at the time, his annoyance was bitter and he felt he had been tricked. 'Would you believe that anyone could have been such a damned fool?' he used to ask wryly. Still, his sons were there in Paris with them, and 'the boys' brought out in him a warmth of affection that few people could have divined beneath his mask of coldness. And among the fashionable society that chattered and intrigued in the elegant salons of the capital, there was no lack of pretty women who surrendered to the Duke more easily that had any beleaguered Peninsular garrison.

14. **TOP LEFT**: *One of Wellington's despatches at Waterloo.*
(*By permission of the Victoria and Albert Museum.*)

15. **TOP RIGHT**: *One of Wellington's despatches at Waterloo.*
(*By permission of the Victoria and Albert Museum.*)

16. **BOTTOM LEFT**: *The Duchess of Wellington, from the original drawing by Lawrence.*
(*By permission of the Mansell Collection.*)

17. **BOTTOM RIGHT**: *The Duke of Wellington, from the miniature by Isabey, 1818.*
(*By permission of the Wallace Collection.*)

I see that the fire has communicated from the Hay stack to the Roof of the Chateau. You must however still keep your Men in those parts to which the fire does not reach. Take care that no Men are lost by the falling in of the Roof or floors—After they both have fallen in occupy the Ruined walls inside of the Garden ; particularly if it should be possible for the Enemy to pass through the Embers in the Inside of the House.

We ought to have more of the Cavalry between the two high Roads. That is to say three Brigades at least besides the Brigade in observation on the Right; & besides the Belgian Cavalry & the D. of Cumberland's Hussars.

One heavy & one light Brigade might remain on the left.

The winter of 1814 found the Duke at the Congress of Vienna, where the victorious nations met to work out an agreement on the new shape of Europe. He had a heavy cold, and complained: 'The hot rooms here have almost killed me.' The heating arrangements at the Congress were not, however, to trouble him long, for in March came the shattering news that Napoleon had escaped from Elba. Diplomatic manoeuvres were turned overnight into frantic attempts to get an army together and to find out where Napoleon was likely to strike. The tenacious Corsican landed near Cannes and marched in triumph across France, rekindling on the way all the flames of enthusiasm everyone had thought extinguished for ever. King Louis XVIII slipped off his throne and discreetly made his way over the border into Lille. Napoleon installed himself again as Emperor of the French and the long shadows began once more to creep up over Europe.

The representatives of the countries which had met at Vienna declared Napoleon to be an outlaw. They put the Duke and the Prussian Marshal Blücher in charge of an Allied army assembled near Brussels. The Peninsular forces had since been dispersed, and in their place the Duke was to command a hastily formed band consisting chiefly of British, Prussian, Dutch and Belgian troops. One day in March the Duke went out for a walk in the park at Brussels. Spring had come early that year, but he gave little thought to the violets that bloomed everywhere in profusion. Intelligence reports had told him that Napoleon was organizing a huge army and that the workshops of Paris were turning out vast quantities of guns and ammunition by night and day. There were misty tales of threatening troop movements along the frontier, and information trickled through that the Imperial Army was marching north. The Duke weighed up the chances of his own 'infamous army, weak and ill-equipped', pitted against a force composed of veterans and inspired by a fierce veneration for their commander. As he walked beside the trim flower beds he met an acquaintance who put a question to him.

'Will you let me ask you, Duke, what you think you will make of it?'

'By God!' he replied, 'I think Blücher and myself can do the thing.'

Then he chanced to see a British private wandering nearby and looking at the statues in the park.

'There!' he barked, pointing at the soldier. 'It all depends upon that article whether we do the business or not. Give me enough of it, and I am sure.'

The days passed by in a cloud of uneasy rumour and flurries of activity. The early part of June was spent in strengthening fortifications and reconnoitring the land around Brussels. On June 15 Napoleon crossed the frontier and rode through cheering crowds to the Belgian town of Charleroi. That evening in Brussels the Duchess of Richmond gave a ball. Byron later re-created the atmosphere:

> There was a sound of revelry by night,
> And Belgium's capital had gathered then
> Her beauty and her chivalry, and bright
> The lamps shone o'er fair women and brave men . . .

The Duke was there, bland, inscrutable, making polite conversation and seeming to enjoy the music and the dancing. A despatch was brought to him, and after he had read it he fell deep in thought. He gave a few brief orders to his staff officers, and apparently returned to his earlier carefree mood. Outside the ballroom the smooth strain of violins was drowned in the martial noise of drums, bagpipes and bugles sounding the call to arms.

At eight o'clock next morning he rode out with his staff through the empty cobbled streets and made for the vital crossroads of Quatre Bras, eleven or so miles from Charleroi. An English maid, rising early to open the shutters, caught a glimpse of him as he swept by, and she cried to her employer: 'O my lady, get up quick; there he goes, God bless him, and he will not come back till he is King of France!' The Duke himself was less sanguine. He inspected Blücher's position at Ligny. He did not like it. 'If they fight there, they will be damnably mauled,' he said, as he returned to his own men at Quatre Bras. He was right. Within a few hours the Imperial Army charged along screaming '*Vive l'Empereur!*' and the Prussians had been thrown out of Ligny. 'Old Blücher has had a damned good hiding . . .' commented the Duke briefly.

The British troops held fast at Quatre Bras, though the Prussians' reverse meant that they had to fall back to a better position near the village of Waterloo. Napoleon failed to press this advantage home, and the Duke as a result gained a valuable breathing space.

He watched the retreat astride his charger Copenhagen, and when the men were safely in position he hurried back to lay plans for the coming battle. Then he spread a newspaper over his face and calmly fell asleep.

The engagement was to be his first direct confrontation with Napoleon. He had little regard for Napoleon the man, whom he thought to be '. . . low and ungentlemanlike. I suppose the narrowness of his early prospects and habits stuck to him. What we understand by gentlemanlike feelings he knew nothing at all about.' He never made the mistake of underestimating Napoleon the brilliant soldier. On the other hand, Napoleon always professed great scorn for the Duke. 'Because you've been beaten by Wellington, you think he's a great general,' he rebuked Marshal Soult at Waterloo. 'I'm telling you he's a bad one. . . .' So bitter was his dislike that he was to bequeath a large sum of money to a Frenchman who once tried to assassinate the Duke. His attitude is a contrast with the Duke's. At one point during the Battle of Waterloo Napoleon came within personal range of the Duke's staff. 'I think I can reach him, may I fire?' asked an officer. 'No, no,' said the Duke, 'Generals commanding armies have something else to do than to shoot at one another.'

A summer storm raged all through the night of June 17 and drenching rain made the camp fires splutter and hiss. 'I never get wet if I can help it,' remarked the Duke as he phlegmatically put on a cloak. Water beat down through the canvas and made the dye of the soldiers' uniforms run. Sunday, June 18, dawned pale and damp. A shower of drizzle went on falling from leaden clouds as the two armies breakfasted in sodden discomfort. Slowly the British moved into position under the feeble gleam of a pallid sun. Among them rode the Duke in his familiar dark blue coat and white cravat. He waited, cannily, for Napoleon to attack first.

It was not until after eleven o'clock that the assault came, for the monsoon-like rains had turned fields into quagmires and paths into streams of mud in which it was almost impossible to manoeuvre cannon. By this time Marshal Blücher, who had recovered from his defeat at Ligny, where he had nearly been crushed to death under his dying horse, was ready for battle again and promising new reinforcements for the Duke. Reeking of gin and rhubarb medicine, he embraced the Duke's liaison officer and cheerily

18. TOP: *The Defence of Hougoumont.* *(By permission of the Scottish United Services Museum.)*

19. BOTTOM: *The 95th Rifles at Waterloo, from the watercolour by K. M. Clayton.*
*(By permission of the National Army Museum.)*

explained: 'I'm afraid I stink a bit!' At half-past eleven the French army advanced into the narrow little patch of ground, no more than three square miles in extent, where the battle was to be decided. The Duke had concealed a strong detachment of his men just beneath the ridge of Mont Saint Jean. To his right was another position at the château of Hougoumont, while he had placed another garrison at the farm of La Haye Sainte in the valley below. 'We shall sleep tonight in Brussels!' exulted Napoleon as he ordered a division to attack Hougoumont. The black hordes of infantry surged upon the outworks and were pushed back again and again, each time leaving a mound of dying men to be finished off among the quick flash of bayonets. But Hougoumont did not fall. At half-past one the Emperor's batteries opened up a violent cannonade which caused more noise than harm, since the Duke's forces had chosen their sheltered positions with care. And now a Prussian contingent was biting deep into Napoleon's flank, leading him to use up valuable reserves of infantry which he sorely needed at other vital points.

The Duke himself, as always, seemed to be everywhere at once. 'The sight of his long nose among us was worth ten thousand men any day of the week,' said one of his troops. He galloped up and down the lines issuing orders: 'Now, gentlemen, for the honour of the Household Troops' – or offering congratulations: 'Life Guards! I thank you,' as he raised his cocked hat with his usual grave courtesy and rode off amid the crack and rattle of musketry in an atmosphere thick with the smell of gunpowder. He personally rallied a detachment of infantry and re-formed them within yards of a French charge that came thundering down. His coolness never deserted him. 'By God! I've lost my leg!' gasped his brother-in-law who happened to be beside him. The shell had whistled close by the Duke and grazed Copenhagen's chestnut flank. 'Have you, by God!' replied the Duke indifferently among the hail of shot that fell about him. His own life that day seemed to be protected as if by some magic charm.

Now the heavy cavalry plunged down the hill. The skirl of bagpipes rose implacably above the hideous din of cannon-shot, and the Scots Greys dashed and slashed among the French with roars of 'Scotland forever!' They pounded over a swampy field as far as the enemy guns. 'Such slaughtering!' recalled one of the survivors. ' . . . I can hear the Frenchmen yet crying "*Diable!*" when I struck at them, and the long-drawn hiss through their teeth as my sword went home.' The battle see-sawed agonizingly through the long dark hours of the afternoon while the French dead piled up around the impregnable slope of Mont Saint Jean. 'Never did I see such a pounding match,' said the Duke. Soon after six o'clock, however, the Duke's position at La Haye Sainte was taken after murderous fighting along the very passages of the farmhouse. Napoleon decided to make a final bid for mastery. He ordered the flower of his army, the Imperial Guard, to advance. These veterans, whose appearance at previous battles had always been the prelude to a glorious victory, swung jauntily along the road to cheers from French wounded who lay in the ditches. They loomed up through the dense clouds of gunsmoke at a visibility of little more than eighty yards. For a moment the smoke lifted and the Guards peered in bafflement at what seemed to be empty ground ahead of them.

In that eerie silence Wellington's deep voice was heard: 'Up Guards, ready.'

The Brigade of Guards suddenly rose from their hiding place and poured a withering volley into the startled ranks of the French. The lines of bearskins wavered for a moment, then staggered on. Another teeming fusillade sent them scattering in confusion. They turned and fled down the slope, to be pursued in hand-to-hand fighting. At every point the Emperor's troops began to falter. An English officer asked the Duke in which direction to attack. 'Right ahead, to be sure,' he grunted.

Sunset went practically unnoticed in a sky clouded with the acrid smoke of cannon. The battle turned into a rout and the French army fled in disorder. They were chased by the Prussians who, in their bloodlust, sabred every living thing they encountered on their headlong charge. In a moonlit wood Napoleon wept as the slow and unwilling realization of defeat came upon him. Night fell on a battlefield strewn with the carcasses of horses and the bodies of tens of thousands of men. Peasants who skulked abroad for loot were implored by dying soldiers in their agony to put them out of misery. Corpses floated in the little streams, jammed up the drinking wells, and lay heaped in jagged piles beneath the trees. Over fields and plains the Prussians drove relentlessly on

*Napoleon Bonaparte, from the painting by Robert Lefevre. (Wellington Museum).*

*The Black Watch at Bay, Quatre Bras 16 June, 1815, from the painting by W. B. Wollen, R.I.* (Rep

TOP LEFT: *The First Marquess of Anglesea, from the painting by Sir Thomas Lawrence.*
(Wellington Museum).

TOP RIGHT: *The Portico Room, Apsley House.* (Wellington Museum).

through the night and slaughtered the fleeing survivors of the once proud Imperial army.

Some time after nine o'clock the Duke met Blücher and discussed the victory. Since neither knew the other's language they spoke, by an unconscious irony, in French. Then, dust-stained and weary, the Duke went back to the cramped little inn that was his headquarters. After close on eighteen hours in the saddle, he dismounted stiffly. Copenhagen lashed out suddenly and narrowly avoided killing him. He was in a mood of black depression. 'In all my life,' he later said, 'I have not experienced such anxiety, for I must confess that I have never been so close to defeat.' He sat down to dinner with his staff officers, and his sadness deepened as he saw the numerous empty seats around the table. 'Those Guards – those Guards, what fine fellows!' he said as the tears rolled down his cheeks. 'Next to a battle lost, the greatest misery is a battle gained.'

He slept little that night, and by dawn he was writing, in his plain and unemphatic style, the famous dispatch to announce the victory. Later in the morning he told an acquaintance: 'It has been a damned serious business. Blücher and I have lost thirty thousand men. It has been a damned nice thing – the nearest run thing you ever saw in your life . . . By God! I don't think it would have been done if I had not been there.' As for himself: 'The finger of Providence was upon me and I escaped unhurt.'

20. *The Battle of Waterloo, from the painting by Sir William Allan.*
*(By permission of the Victoria and Albert Museum.)*

# Prime Minister

21. *The Duke of Wellington, from a painting by Lawrence.*  *(By permission of the Mansell Collection.)*

# 7

Since 1815 historians have re-fought the battle of Waterloo many times on paper. Differing interpretations abound, and it is hard to say whether any one of them is wholly wrong – or wholly right. In the rush and confusion of battle no single man ever knew exactly what was going on. It has, for example, been impossible to establish the precise time of day at which certain major events occurred, for even the most reliable accounts differ. As the Duke himself observed: 'The history of a battle is not unlike the history of a ball. Some individuals may recollect all the little events of which the great result is the battle won or lost; but no individual can recollect the order in which, or the exact moment at which, they occurred, which make all the difference as to their value or importance.'

There is, however, one clear and unassailable test of a general's worth. It is a harsh fact of the soldier's profession that the only successful general is the one who wins battles. Despite the unceasing argument over details, no-one can deny that the Duke won the battle of Waterloo, nor that Napoleon lost it. 'Napoleon did not manoeuvre at all,' said the Duke. 'He just moved forward in the old style, in columns, and was driven off in the old style.' The Duke's partiality for infantry squares, in which an outer ring of men knelt to form an almost impregnable barrier of bayonets while from inside the square another rank fired over their heads at the enemy, was a powerful factor in his victory. It was a tactic that had proved its worth during the Peninsular campaign. Indeed, his career, viewed as a whole, seems to have been one long preparation for the crowning triumph of Waterloo. India and the Peninsular had taught him the value of carefully planned defensive action. That was one side of his nature. The other side was shown in the sudden strikes which caught the enemy off balance, for there was in his character an impulsiveness, a hare-brained readiness to gamble against seemingly fantastic odds, which self-discipline kept under control until the moment for reckless-ness appeared.

Less than a month after Waterloo Napoleon surrendered. The 'Hundred Days' of his return to power ended and his final exile to St Helena began. The Duke took up command of the Army of Occupation in Paris, where his achievements, though not as spectacular as in war, were hardly less formidable. He had to ensure the stability of the régime under the newly-restored King Louis XVIII and to steer the country away from the dangers of a civil war. His diplomacy was needed to prevent the vengeful Prussians from exacting huge and vindictive reparations and even from blowing up a Paris bridge named after one of Napoleon's victories over them. Still more complicated were the negotiations to create new European boundaries after Napoleon's ventures and to return to their rightful owners the quantities of loot that his armies had brought back from their conquests.

In all these matters the Duke stood out among the leaders of foreign governments who came to the conferences in Paris. His prestige was infinite and he became the most important man in Europe. The British army and the British nation also benefited from the Duke's reflected glory, and for a time his power was such that he could have done almost anything he wanted. Yet he remained as clear-headed as he always had been. His decisions were moderate, his actions dictated by common-sense alone, and he never allowed revenge or self-seeking to taint his judgement. He was human enough, though, to enjoy the splendid social life that came his way. While his wife stayed quietly in England, he entertained kings, princes and prime ministers at grand receptions where Kitty would decidedly have been out of place. Gossip about his bachelor existence went so far as to link his name with a beautiful opera singer who charmed Paris audiences of the time.

It was too much to expect the French to like the man who had beaten them. He was unpopular alike with those who still hankered after Napoleon and with supporters of the new régime. At a reception one evening all the marshals present turned their backs on him. The king started an embarrassed apology. 'Sire,' replied the Duke, 'do not distress yourself. They've so got into the habit of showing me their backs that they can't get out of it.' Even his enemies appreciated the wit.

The Duke's unpopularity was increased by the affair of Marshal Ney. This brave and impulsive soldier had thrown in his lot with Louis XVIII in 1814. When the King sent him, in 1815, to turn back the advancing Napoleon, he changed sides again. Soon after Waterloo he was, by a mischance, flushed out of his hiding place and sentenced to death for treason. The Duke was asked to intervene. He refused. He did not wish, he explained, to be accused of meddling in 'the workings of the French King's Government. . . .' Such was the hatred Wellington incurred that in 1816 an attempt was made to burn him alive in his house. Two years later a would-be assassin fired at him by the guttering light of an oil lamp as he came home from a party. But 'the finger of God' was upon the Duke and he emerged unharmed.

In his leisure hours he continued to play the host to travelling celebrities. Among his English visitors were Sir Walter Scott, whom he helped in his biography of Napoleon by supplying an account of the Russian campaign; the actress Sarah Siddons; Lady Shelley, the sister of the poet; and many other famous people who came to tour the field of Waterloo, and then went on to Paris to pay him their respects. They would find him waiting to receive them in his blue coat with metal buttons, a white cravat fastened with a silver buckle, black breeches and silk stockings. Under his left knee was the Order of the Garter, and around his neck blazed the Golden Fleece. He was affable and good-natured. For the benefit of admiring ladies he would often demonstrate how he fought the battle of Waterloo – though observers noted with amusement that over the years the numbers of the enemy tended to increase.

By the end of 1818 there was little left for the Duke to do in France. The government seemed reasonably stable, and the thorny problem of how much compensation France was to pay countries who had suffered from Napoleonic ambition was finally settled with the exercise of much tact and patience. In between times the Duke carried out many useful missions, not least of which was the purchase of a beautiful house in the rue du Faubourg Saint-Honoré for use as the British Embassy. He bought it from Pauline Borghese, one of Napoleon's sisters, and the Embassy it has remained to this day. When the British Ambassador holds a banquet, the guests are still served on plate that once belonged to Pauline.

In the last winter months of the year the Duke was back in England for good. There was not much more his countrymen could do to honour him. He was now a Field Marshal in all the armies of Europe, the holder of innumerable foreign titles, and a landowner in several different countries. The House of Commons voted him two hundred and sixty-three thousand pounds to buy an estate at Stratfield Saye in Hampshire. He grew to love the place and showed himself a model landlord. He was for ever improving his property, repairing the homes and farms of his tenants, and ploughing back the profits into the estate. 'I do this,' he remarked, 'out of consideration for future Dukes of Wellington.' On one occasion his agent bought some adjoining land at a very low price and told him of the bargain they had. The Duke would have none of it, and the crestfallen agent was sent back to pay the vendor the difference between the selling price and the real value of the land.

At about the same time the Duke bought from his brother Richard a London home at Hyde Park Corner. It was called Apsley House, now the Wellington Museum. It was known as 'Number One, London,' since it was the first house a traveller would pass at that time on entering London from the west. The Duke spent large sums of money on decorating and transforming it to his taste – larger sums, indeed, than he ever intended, for by the time the architects and builders had finished with it he was complaining bitterly at having to pay well over forty thousand pounds for the work done. One of his most impressive additions was the long and spacious room known as the Waterloo Gallery. Here, in after years, on 18 June, he used to hold the famous Waterloo Banquets which were attended by generals and officers who had fought under him. Upon the table stood the Portuguese dinner service, a monumental centre piece twenty-six feet long and consisting of about a thousand items in silver and silver gilt. It may be seen there still today, a gleaming reminder of those evenings long ago when the Duke lived again, with the men he had commanded, the greatest event of his career.

He was fifty years old and in the prime of life. His hair was becomingly grey, his eye twinkled with frosty intelligence, and his slim figure, dressed in neat and well-tailored clothes, recalled his earlier nickname of 'the Beau'. The England he had known was changing fast. Like all wartime Cabinets faced with the problems of peace, Lord Liverpool's Tory administration was beset with difficulties. The Duke was a national asset too useful to waste, and he was invited to join the Cabinet as Master General of the Ordnance. It was a conveniently vague appointment that enabled his colleagues to profit from his advice on a wide variety of questions. There was no-one to approach him for experience of foreign affairs, and his vast knowledge was constantly being pressed into service. On home affairs it was different. The Duke was a soldier who had spent most of his career abroad. The England of his youth was rapidly passing away, and his attitudes were rooted in ideas that were twenty years out of date. Moreover, his military training had taught him to support the orderly preservation of institutions as they were. Anything else savoured of revolution. He therefore viewed the stirrings of modern democracy with grave concern. For the Duke was a product of the eighteenth century, and it was a long time before people realized that Waterloo, instead of marking the beginning of a new age, represented for once and all the burial of an old one.

The government, too, had made a mistake in pinning its hopes on a man whose popularity a few short years ago had been unassailable. In the general unrest now sweeping England the

Duke became the embodiment of reaction. Riding in Hyde Park one day he was hooted by the crowd. They ran away when he pulled up his horse, but the experience was unpleasant. That same year an attempt was made to murder all the members of the Cabinet. It was called the Cato Street Conspiracy after the place where the conspirators were arrested, and it ended in failure. Yet it had shown the bleak discontent that was caused by unemployment. The Duke suggested that ministers all carry pistols with them. Perhaps it was as well that the idea was not carried out, for he himself was a poor shot and more of a danger to his colleagues than any assassin. Out shooting one day he succeeded in peppering a dog, a keeper, and an elderly cottager. The poor lady understandably protested. 'My good woman,' replied the Duke's companion, 'this ought to be the proudest moment of your life, you have had the distinction of being shot by the great Duke of Wellington!' The Duke slipped his victim a guinea.

In 1821 the dissolute Prince Regent at last came to the throne as George IV. The Duke was at his coronation dressed in all his glory as Lord High Constable. 'By God!' the Duke exclaimed once, 'you never saw such a figure in your life as he is. Then he speaks and swears so like old Falstaff, that damn me if I was not ashamed to walk into a room with him.' The much-maligned George IV left behind him as his monument the extravagant architecture of Brighton Pavilion and the layout of Regent's Park. He was a difficult man to deal with, and of all his ministers only the Duke was really able to handle him. When Lord Castlereagh went mad and committed suicide after ten years as Foreign Secretary, it was the Duke who persuaded the king to accept Canning, a very able politician, as his successor. Now the king detested Canning, for the latter had refused to support him in his harsh treatment of Queen Caroline. Canning, said the king, had hurt his feelings as a gentleman.

'You're not a gentleman, sir,' remarked the Duke.

'Not a gentleman!!!' exclaimed the astonished George IV.

'No, sir, you are King of England, and have to carry out his duties.'

If the Duke was unpopular as a politician, he remained the favourite objective of writers, portrait painters and sculptors. 'I have been much exposed to authors,' he would complain as he answered for the hundreth time some request from a biographer for details of Waterloo. Every post brought begging letters, appeals for testimonials and demands for help. Until the day of his death he answered them all in his own handwriting. Some mornings he would write as many as fifty letters and notes, for he was so quick a penman that he could cover a sheet of paper before the ink was dry. 'The Duke presents his compliments,' was how he usually began, choosing the third person as if to indicate that he wrote not as a personal acquaintance – since, indeed, most of his correspondents were totally unknown to him – but as a public figure doing his duty. He was a master of the crushing snub. 'F. M. the Duke of Wellington presents his compliments to Mr Oliver,' he once wrote. 'He declares distinctly that he knows nothing of Mr Edward Oliver, and that he is astonished at the insolence of any person requiring him to certify to Messrs. Coutts & Co., [the bankers] or any other person, that of which the person who makes the requisition must know that the Duke has no personal knowledge.' Mr Oliver was duly put in his place. Nevertheless, the Duke often wrote so gruffly that the recipient of his letter, believing his request for a favour to have been turned down, would be surprised a few days later to find that the Duke had in fact used his influence on his behalf. The old soldiers who came up to him at railway stations claiming to be veterans of Waterloo could always rely on a guinea.

Among the artists lucky enough to persuade the Duke to 'sit' for them was David Wilkie. The Duke paid him £1,260, laboriously counting out the notes by hand. Wilkie thought it would save trouble to write a cheque.

'Do you think I like Coutts' clerks always to know how foolishly I spend my money?' grunted the Duke.

Another artistic project that had his approval was the large bronze statue of Achilles, eighteen feet high, which was put up as a tribute to him in Hyde Park on the Waterloo anniversary of 1822. That same year his left ear-drum was shattered in the course of a firing practice at Woolwich. A well-known aurist treated the ear by syringing it with a strong solution of caustic. 'I don't think I ever suffered so much in my life,' said the Duke. 'It was not pain; it was something far worse.' He would have died if another doctor had not treated him immediately. The unfortunate aurist, seeing his career in ruins, was gently reassured: 'Don't say a word about it; you acted for the best; it has been unfortunate, no doubt, for both of us, but you are not at all to blame.' From this time onwards the Duke no longer enjoyed his usual excellent health. His opinion of doctors became sceptical: 'I am put to torture with blisters, only because they will do me no harm; and then I am to be told that doctors are not *charlatans*,' he wrote angrily. 'You know as well as I do that they are! and that what they talk is neither more nor less than *nonsense and stuff. . . .*'

Still suffering from the ill effects of the misguided ear treatment, he travelled to Verona as Britain's representative at the last of the great Congresses. The following year an attack of inflammation left him a weakly prey to cholera. But he never allowed illness to keep him away from duty, and like the General de Gaulle of a later age he always appeared at ceremonial occasions in impeccable uniform while everyone else was closely muffled up against foul weather. The most he would admit was: 'I was a little out of sorts, but I'm all right now.'

The winter of 1826 brought him to St Petersburg on a mission to the new Tsar of Russia. The Duke saw no reason to refuse when the task was offered him. Though prone to dizziness and occasional fainting, he was undaunted by the hardships of a long journey such as this, and he faced up cheerfully to the vermin that infested the coaching posts, the snow, the ice and the cold that penetrated everywhere. He even survived Russian hospitality which mainly comprised 'pallid asparagus and foetid oysters', and returned to London with cause for satisfaction at his diplomacy. The political scene, however, was cloudy. Lord Liverpool, the Prime Minister, suffered a stroke and his government broke up. Canning took his place and quarrelled hotly with the Duke. Appointed Commander-in-Chief of the army only a few months before, the Duke smartly resigned in a flash of Irish hotheadedness. By the middle of 1827 Canning, too, had died and the government was looking for another Prime Minister.

Who was it to be? For a few months the vague figure of Lord Goderich presided, shadow-like, at the head. Then a fit of apoplexy removed him from the scene and the post was vacant again. A Royal summons arrived for the Duke. He found the king in bed, a greasy turban adorning his locks and a shabby silk nightdress crumpled about his fat body. 'Arthur,' said the monarch, 'the Cabinet is defunct.' The Duke left Windsor with instructions to form a government.

He had lost none of his relish for official business, and soon he was happily engulfed in the contents of the red despatch boxes that clamoured for attention. Having reached the top of his profession as Commander of the British army, he had now gained the highest post open to a civilian. He rarely kept anyone waiting for a decision – his dislike of hesitancy sometimes even made him give the wrong one out of a wish for speedy administration. But if the Duke was Prime Minister, he was by no means a politician. Accustomed as a soldier to issue orders and to see them promptly obeyed by his subordinates, he was vexed by the apparent unruliness of political colleagues who disagreed with him. 'What is the meaning of a party if they don't follow their leaders?' he thundered. 'Damn 'em! let 'em go!' Go they often did, for when his ministers flourished the politician's ultimate deterrent and offered their resignation, the Duke flabbergasted them by calmly accepting it.

It is often difficult for later generations to understand why the political controversies of a bygone era should in their time have aroused such passion. One of the most hotly argued problems which the Duke had to face was that of Catholic Emancipation. Since Britain was officially a Protestant country, the Test Act of the seventeenth century forbade Catholics to hold public office. Little had been done in the years between to end this discrimination. The issue had now come to a head, especially in Ireland, where the patriot Daniel O'Connell organized a movement which could well mean civil war. Wellington disliked the idea of Catholic Emancipation. So did his Home Secretary, Robert Peel. But the Duke, whose practical realism was nowhere more apparent than on this occasion, clearly saw the dangers of mishandling an inflammable situation. In 1829 he introduced the Repeal of the Test Act.

George IV bitterly opposed the idea. 'Damn it, you mean to let them into Parliament?' he complained. For hours on end the Duke had to bear with being talked at by an excited and indignant monarch who even threatened to abdicate. In the end Royalty capitulated. The Tory peers who disapproved of the measure remained to be handled and people wondered how the Duke would set about it. 'Oh, that will be simple enough,' somebody remarked. 'He'll say, "My lords! Attention! Right about face! Quick march!" and the thing will be done.' Put in simple terms, that is just about what happened.

The bill did not go through without creating personal enmities. The Earl of Winchilsea, an ardent Protestant, was foolish enough to attack Wellington's private character. The Duke had no alternative. One misty morning in Battersea Fields, now Battersea Park, the two men arrived to fight a duel. It was the first the Duke had ever undertaken.

'Now then, Hardinge,' he observed to his second, 'look sharp and step out the ground. I have no time to waste. Damn it! don't stick him up so near the ditch. If I hit him, he will tumble in.'

The duellists took aim. 'Fire!' said a voice. The Duke hit Winchilsea's coat. His opponent fired in the air. The Duke raised two fingers to the brim of his hat, wished everyone a polite 'Good morning,' and rode away. Jeremy Bentham, the philosopher, sent him a letter which began 'Ill-advised Man,' and rebuked him for risking his life so unwisely. 'Compliments. The Duke has received his letter,' was the stately reply.

The issue of Catholic Emancipation was a triumph for the Duke. With the other great question which faced his government he was totally unsuccessful. This was the topic of Parliamentary Reform. He did not see the necessity for changing a system of Parliamentary representation which social developments in the nineteenth century had made out-of-date and unrealistic. The fact that a large population had grown up without the right to vote seemed to him an admirable reason for preserving the system. Once you took away the power of the traditional governing class, he argued, you were opening the door to anarchy and the mob. He knew what mobs were all about. Mobs were soldiers who plundered and got drunk unless they were disciplined. Mobs were disorganized civilians who roamed the streets and damaged private property. The Whig party supported Reform and this clinched the matter for him. By his birth, upbringing and experience of life the Duke was a Tory. The Whigs were the people who, during the Peninsular War, had attacked him in Parliament and hoped that he would be defeated by Napoleon. His position was clear.

Soon after the Test Act had been repealed, demand for Reform began to grow. It quickly became an irresistible force. The Duke refused to give way and enraged its advocates with stark defiance. He foresaw, rightly, that it would finish by eroding the influence of the aristocracy, the Church, and the great land owners. The storm whirled viciously around his head and made him the most unpopular man in Britain. His government fell, the Duke was out of office, and for the next few years he fought a hard but losing battle against Reform in opposition. The 1830 revolution in France served only to strengthen his belief in the danger of mob rule.

It was a dark period in his life. One April evening in 1831 a rebellious crowd threw stones at the windows of Apsley House. They did not know that within the gloomy, echoing building the Duke sat in silence beside his dead wife. For Kitty, frail and scatterbrained to the last, had died after ailing for many months 'paler than marble'. He had never been able to return her love. He could not forget that, in despair of arousing his affection, she had set his sons against him. This caused him acute sorrow. 'In fact I can accuse myself of no fault excepting excess of Indulgence,' he had written. 'But I say that it is impossible that they can do that of which they are guilty without being excited to it by their Mother. . . .' A mutual friend recalled: '. . . she made the Duke's children as afraid of speaking openly to him as she was herself. The words "Don't tell your father" were ever on her lips. It seemed to be the one object of her life to pose as a cruelly neglected wife. Unfortunately she succeeded in making that impression upon her eldest son. . . . In consequence, her sons pitied without respecting her.'

Even so, she had been his Duchess. She had borne his children. Now she lay dead in the fading light while angry crowds roared outside and stones shattered the windows and damaged his furniture. They were back again a few days afterwards and a servant drove them off by shooting a blunderbuss in the air. In October the siege was renewed. The Duke told a correspondent: '. . . a Mob surrounded my House, upon which they commenced an attack with stones which lasted 50 Minutes in broad daylight before any assistance came. They broke all the Windows on the lower floor looking towards Rotten Row, a great Number in my

Room in which I was sitting. . . . It is now five o'clock and beginning to rain a little; and I conclude that the Gentlemen will now go to their Dinners!' Wellington, ever practical, had iron shutters fitted and so, as has been suggested, came to be known as 'the Iron Duke'. In later years, when his popularity returned and crowds gathered to cheer him, he would point to the iron shutters and ride off without a word.

The demonstrations persisted. Hisses greeted him whenever he appeared in public and threats of murder were commonplace. In 1832, on June 18, he rode through London pursued by screaming rioters who tried to pull him off his horse and pelted him with stones. He looked straight ahead, as if he were made of 'cast-metal', as Carlyle remarked. He reached Apsley House at last amid a tornado of hysterical booing. It was the seventeenth anniversary of Waterloo. 'An odd day to choose,' observed the Duke as he calmly dismounted.

22. *A Walk by the Seashore, 1832.* *(By permission of the Victoria and Albert Museum.)*

# The Duke

23. *Wellington riding in Hyde Park, 1852.* *(By permission of the Victoria and Albert Museum.)*

8

At some point in the early 1830s the tide of opinion began to run in favour of the Duke. He was no longer a hated politician but an elder statesman, the veteran of a glorious battle and one who had become a living legend. The first sign of this new status appeared when he was installed as Chancellor of Oxford University. A trifle alarmed at the prospect of having to make the traditional address in Latin, he looked for help in what seemed to be the obvious direction: 'Now, any speech is difficult, but a Latin one was impossible; so in this dilemma I applied to my Physician, as most likely, from his prescriptions, to know Latin, and he made me a speech, which answered very well. I believe it was a very good speech, but I did not know much of the matter.' When he entered for the ceremony he was greeted with a frenzied burst of applause that lasted for ten minutes. This was nothing to the pandemonium that broke out at a mention of Waterloo. Hats, caps and handkerchieves were waved, and clouds of dust rose up from stamping feet. Through it all the Duke sat motionless as a statue.

Old passions were dying out, too. He went down to the new Parliament which had been elected after the passing of the Reform Bill he so stoutly opposed. He cast a disapproving eye over the scene. 'I never saw so many shocking bad hats in my life,' he said. Reform was now the law of the land and there was nothing more to be done about it. In any case, he was a very busy man with too much work on his mind to waste time in regretting past defeats. The Chancellorship of Oxford was only one of the many public offices he filled. He was also Governor of Plymouth, Lord Lieutenant of Hampshire, Master of Trinity House, and the holder of many regimental commands. Most men would have been content to regard these honours as pleasant sinecures. The Duke, on the contrary, inspected every detail of administration and made himself detested by officials who had fallen into lazy ways. As Constable of the Tower of London, for example, he struck fear into yeoman warders who had previously let out their dwellings and feathered their nests in other lucrative ways. The chaplain was rebuked for his rare attendances, and the Tower doctor, who erred in similar fashion, was bluntly reprimanded: 'The Medical Gentleman must attend. If he is too old to do his duty he must resign; and I must recommend another.' The Duke certainly gave, and expected, value for money.

Of all his appointments, it was the Lord Wardenship of the Cinque Ports which brought him most pleasure. He was much attached to Walmer Castle, where he liked to dine in the Cinque Ports uniform of blue coat, scarlet collar and blue trousers. The place was, he used to say, 'the most charming marine residence' he had ever seen. Here he would emerge at six in the morning, stroll along the battlements to take the sea air, and then, before discussing the day's business with the Channel pilots, he would as usual tackle a great pile of correspondence.

Life these days fell into a pattern that arranged itself round Apsley House, Stratfield Saye and Walmer Castle. Whenever the Duke could spare the time he would go hunting, appearing in a garb which only he could have carried off: on wet days he turned out on horseback carrying an open umbrella to protect his befurred red frock coat, lilac waistcoat and kid gloves. 'I have seldom seen a man with less idea of riding than he has,' wrote an observer. 'His seat is unsightly in the extreme, and few men get more falls in the course of a year than his Grace. Nevertheless he seems to enjoy the thing amazingly, and what with leading over occasionally and his groom's assistance, he did very well.' He was as reckless on the box of a carriage as he was on horseback, and he drove his curricle along narrow country lanes with an impatient fury that terrified his companions.

'The Duke gets along,' said a friend who had been following on one such trip, 'he soon left me behind.'

'There is no doubt of that,' quavered someone who had travelled in the Duke's carriage, 'I thought more than once that he would have left me behind too.'

He had always been fascinated by mechanical things. The lady guests at Stratfield Saye were sometimes frightened by the threatening hiss of hot-water pipes, for the Duke was an early pioneer of central heating. The proud inventor would show them a new finger bandage he had just perfected, or a murderous sword-umbrella, or a tea-pot which poured automatically. His most ingenious discovery was a device that enabled the user to read a newspaper in the bath without getting the pages wet. In old age he returned to his early love of music and planned concerts with all the care he once devoted to bridging the Douro. He himself chose the programme from among his favourite Mozart and Handel pieces, and he made a point of personally engaging the artists to perform them.

There was a brief political interlude when the Prime Minister of the day resigned and the Duke was called out of retirement to hold the fort while Peel, who was touring Europe, was hasily sent for to come back and form a new government. In the meantime, for three unusual weeks, the Duke ran the country. A witty cartoonist was stating no more than the facts when he listed the temporary Cabinet as follows:

| | |
|---|---|
| First Lord of the Treasury | Duke of Wellington |
| Home Secretary | Duke of Vitoria |
| Foreign Secretary | Prince of Waterloo |
| War and Colonies | Duke of Ciudad Rodrigo |
| Lord Privy Seal | Count Vimeiro |

| | |
|---|---|
| First Lord of the Admiralty | Baron Douro |
| Chancellor of the Exchequer | Arthur Wellesley |
| Lord High Chancellor | Viscount Wellington |

The country looked on its ruler with affectionate amusement. Then Peel came back and the Duke gracefully stepped down to serve as Foreign Secretary in the short-lived government that followed.

Everyone saw that he was really above politics now. Everyone knew who was meant by that simple phrase 'the Duke.' The crowds would gather and shout 'God bless you, Duke!' 'For Heaven's sake, people, let me get on my horse,' he replied with a fine disregard for popularity. Daily he would ride down to the War Office to do his work as Commander-in-Chief of the Army, a post to which he had been re-appointed and which he was to hold for the rest of his life. 'Wearily the right leg scrambled, so to speak, over the croup of the saddle. Slowly and painfully it sank towards the ground, and then the whole body came down with a stagger which was never witnessed but with dismay. Yet nobody presumed to touch or even approach him. Through the open doorway he passed without taking any notice of those about him, and, mounting the steps, made straight for the little room in which he transacted military business.' And still the anecdotes multiplied. An unscrupulous person tried to blackmail him by threatening to publish falsely incriminating documents. 'Publish and be damned!' said the Duke. While strolling in Hyde Park a gentleman came up to him and said: 'Mr Robinson, I presume?' The Duke stared blankly: 'If you believe that, you'd believe anything.'

Yet for all his fame the Duke was a very lonely man. The death of his wife was quickly followed by the loss of his mother at the age of ninety. Neither of them had meant a great deal to him, and he missed the Countess of Mornington even less than Kitty. Over the years her attitude towards him had changed. Whereas she had once regarded him as the dunce of the family, his increasingly distinguished career was hailed by her with such proud expressions as 'our beloved hero; God bless him,' which became, eventually, 'dear Arthur'. Her affection had flowered too late. Clear in his memory was the coldness with which the stern and unsympathetic mother had treated him as a sensitive child, and he never forgave it. He showed more emotion at the death of Copenhagen, the sturdy old chestnut horse which had carried him at Waterloo and at so many other battles. Copenhagen was buried at Stratfield Saye with full military honours.

He lived very simply and quietly. At Stratfield Saye he slept upon a sofa. At Walmer he used a small iron bedstead with a hair mattress, blanket and eiderdown. His bedtime reading consisted chiefly of the Bible, several religious works and Caesar's *Commentaries*. When *The Pickwick Papers* first came out he would read extracts aloud to his visitors with keen enjoyment. The encounter between Wellington and Dickens, between the last of the eighteenth century aristocrats and the first Victorian novelist of the industrial age, was a piquant confrontation in history.

Of course, the Duke had his friends. There was Charles Arbuthnot, a diplomatist whom he had known since the early years of the century. Arbuthnot and his wife became the Duke's closest companions, and the death of Mrs Arbuthnot left both men stricken with grief. At the Duke's suggestion Arbuthnot came to stay with him at Apsley House where the two solitary widowers lived out their days, the Duke fussing over Arbuthnot like a maternal aunt. Arbuthnot fell ill and the doctor reported that there was no hope. The Duke seized the doctor's hand and stroked it pathetically.

'No, no, he's not very ill, not very bad – he'll get better,' he said in broken accents.

The doctor's diagnosis was unhappily correct. The Duke went to the funeral with tears streaming down his face.

'One by one,' it was said, 'all his pleasures have dropped from him like leaves from a tree in winter.' His deafness, now acute, restricted social life, and he filled his need for human companionship in long correspondence with a small circle of women friends. They provided him with the admiration and assurance that he wanted. He also had his grandchildren. Reconciled with his sons, he now looked forward to family visits that brought with them troops of excited little persons who called him 'Mr Dook'. They climbed all over him, were hunted by him on all-fours beneath the dining-room table, and got their reward in the form of shilling-pieces hung on ribbon – blue for those who wanted to go into the Navy when they were grown up, and scarlet for the Army.

'How d'ye do, Duke?' they would chatter. 'I want some tea, Duke.'

'You shall have it,' came the answer, 'if you promise not to slop it over me, as you did yesterday.'

Each evening there was a pillow fight which was christened, inevitably, 'the battle of Waterloo'. A visitor to Walmer Castle was disturbed one day to see the Duke scampering over the ramparts in pursuit of a little girl shouting: 'I'll catch ye! Ha, ha, I've got ye!' His affection extended to children outside the family as well, and a neighbour's offspring, when caught by the Duke's butler plundering his orchard, spoke up: 'Never mind, let's go to the Duke; he always allows everything and gives you what you like directly.'

A reminder of the doting grandfather's past battles hung heavy in the air at the coronation of the young Queen Victoria. France was represented by Marshal Soult, who had survived Napoleon's defeat and had later risen to high office under the new régime. As the French Ambassador Extraordinary he met the Duke at Buckingham Palace, and the two old warriors fell into long discussion of their campaigns. Soult frequently came to Apsley House and met the Duke's Peninsular generals. 'What! have I found you at last?' he joked to one of the commanders who had skilfully eluded him in retreating from Madrid. 'You, whom I followed so long without ever being able to overtake you.' The Duke even proposed a toast to Soult at a Mansion House banquet. When, however, he was asked to toast the French Army, his amiability vanished.

'No, by God,' he roared, 'we'll beat 'em, but dammee, we won't drink to 'em!'

The Duke's last military manoeuvre took place in London. At one time the agitations of the Chartists, a group demanding political reform, became so violent that the government was seriously frightened. The Chartists intended to march on London and to hold a giant demonstration there. The Duke was called in to organize the defence of the capital. 'His old eyes sparkled like a girl's at her first ball,' remarked someone who watched him planning defensive positions and laying out his forces. This return to the campaigning atmosphere of earlier days made him feel young once more, and although, fortunately, the Chartists never reached London, the Duke enjoyed excitements which he had thought never to meet again.

As Commander-in-Chief of the Army he got through his work with speed and clarity. His astonishing memory, his intimate command of detail and his gift for accurately summing up character were qualities that had been rare indeed among authority in the days when Arthur Wellesley suffered from incompetent superiors. The Duke has sometimes been accused of laying a dead hand on the army. There are those who say he retarded its development to such an extent that the forces who left England to fight in 1914 were modelled largely on his own Peninsular expedition. It is true, also, that he was suspicious of obvious 'cleverness' and so was partly responsible for the tradition of officers who did what they were told and asked no questions. The answer to these criticisms is that the Duke had no clear-cut system or 'school' to indoctrinate his successors. He viewed each problem on its merits and solved it in his own unique fashion. When he died there was no-one of his stature who could do the same, and it is hardly fair to blame him for the fact that those who came after lacked his brilliance and failed to adapt the army to changing conditions. His insistence on the need for a soldier to have the widest possible background, as opposed to the occasionally narrow training received at military colleges, was among the most important maxims he bequeathed to posterity. He summarized the qualities a soldier needs as follows: 'An officer in the British army is not a mere fighting machine. He may be called upon any day to serve the crown as governor of a colony, or in disturbed districts as a magistrate; and he will not be able to fill either post well, unless he knows something of the constitution and laws of the land.'

Even in old age the Duke was never allowed to forget that he was a public figure. Every morning his letter box was full to overflowing. 'It is quite curious with what a number of Insane persons I am in relation,' he mused. 'Mad retired officers, Mad Women . . .' Among them was a slightly deranged young lady of the name of Jenkins. She sought to save the Duke's eternal soul from damnation, and he, with his usual punctiliousness, answered her exhortations by return of post. She came to Apsley House and read the Bible to him. She prayed for him ostentatiously and snowed him under with tracts, hymns and religious publications.

For over twenty years the strange acquaintanceship waxed and waned. At one period Miss Jenkins fully believed that she was to be the next Duchess of Wellington. She was soon disillusioned. The Duke's genuine interest in religion was not of the sort to bind him to a dotty encumbrance such as Miss Jenkins, and in the end the wild epistles of the thirty-three-year-old missionary were left unanswered by her eighty-year-old quarry.

Miss Jenkins was one of out many hundreds of correspondents, from Prime Ministers to impecunious tradesmen, who looked to the Duke for the solution of their troubles. 'Rest!' he exclaimed. 'Every other animal – even a donkey, a costermonger's donkey – is allowed some rest, but the Duke of Wellington never! There is no help for it. As long as I am able to go on, they put a saddle on my back and make me go.... It is like everything else. Nobody else will do it. The Duke of Wellington *must*.' Every charitable body in Europe regarded him as fair game for subscriptions to the building of new schools, hospitals and almshouses. Though his replies were invariably cold, it was not often that they disappointed. Orphanages, in particular, could rely on contributions from him, since, as he said with a grim reference to his warlike past, he had been 'the involuntary means of making many orphans, and therefore was bound to do what he could to provide for them.' Arbuthnot once found him at his desk putting bundles of banknotes into envelopes.

'What are you doing, Duke?' enquired Arbuthnot.

'Doing?' he replied. 'Doing what I am obliged to do every day. It would take the wealth of the Indies to meet all the demands that are made on me.' Although he complained, he readily gave large sums to deserving causes despite his awareness that on many occasions he was being tricked. He preferred to keep his faith in human nature intact. As his brother once said to him: 'You care less about money than any man I ever met with'.

However much he grumbled at the demands made on him, he would have been unhappy without anything to do. He was up at dawn every morning, believing that 'when it's time to turn over it's time to turn out!' This habit of early rising, begun when he was a young officer in India, had given him, somebody once calculated 'almost exactly seven years of wakefulness and, constituted as he was, of activity'. Together with his custom of mapping out the day's engagements with such precision that he never needed to check the time by his watch, his early rising helps to explain the enormous quantity of work he was always able to complete. His correspondence done, he would go out for a ride in the Park, '. . . to the last a spare lithe figure, smart as a young boy, dressed with a scrupulous neatness, and even a tinge of dandyism, in a tight-fitting, single breasted blue frock coat, with spotless white trousers. When he passed all men doffed their hats to him as if he had been a king, and the answering salute of the forefinger raised to the brim of his hat, never omitted, never varying, became almost historic. . . .'

He regularly appeared in his seat at the House of Lords and followed the proceedings as intently as his deafness would allow. He was there at the announcement of a new administration; as each name was read out he turned to his neighbour grunting: 'Who? Who?' The government became known as the 'Who? Who? Ministry.' Sometimes he made a speech, and though, with all his hummings and hawings, he had never been a great orator, he said what he had to say, bluntly and plainly, and then sat down.

On Sundays, whether in the country or in London, he never missed church service. His religion was straightforward. The Lord's Prayer, he said, 'contained the sum total of religion and of morals.' Congregations were fascinated with the vision of his white hair lit by the sunlight streaming through stained-glass windows. But unless the sermon was particularly good, he would settle himself comfortably in the corner of his pew and fall asleep with loud snores.

He had firm ideas about diet. In his last years he was practically a teetotaller and food lost all interest for him. His recipe for curing a cold was to starve himself for days on end, and he often went hunting after a breakfast that consisted of nothing but dry biscuit. Another favourite remedy was to put on rubber gloves and rub himself briskly with vinegar and water. One of his women correspondents was told: 'You have never had a cold since I gave you gloves, and advised you to rub yourself with Vinegar and Water, nor have I one that signified. My ears are tender so that I am constantly catching cold, but it is never of any consequence, I rub with Vinegar and Water and it all goes off!' Doctors were only to be called in when serious illness threatened. The Duke, from hard experience, distrusted medical men.

The throne of England, whose occupants he had known intimately for many years, was filled now by a young woman half a century younger than he was. He thought she could not have performed her duties better had she been his daughter. His favourable feeling was not at first reciprocated. Early in Victoria's reign there had been trouble over her relations with Peel, then Prime Minister, and the Duke, as usual, had been called in to mediate. There were more disagreements when Victoria announced her decision to marry Prince Albert. The Duke's diplomacy in the matter went unappreciated, and the queen, asked if he would be invited to the wedding, snapped: 'What! That old rebel! I won't have him.' He came in the end, and gradually their association improved until she could write of him as 'a true, kind friend and a most valuable adviser'. He stood paternally close to her at ceremonies, was an unfailing guest at royal christenings, and often stayed at Windsor Castle where he loyally concealed the fact that the draught-swept rooms invariably gave him a cold. 'I thought that I should never get warm in the first night that I slept there,' he commented.

The Queen, in return, honoured him with visits to his country home and to Walmer Castle. He viewed the prospect with mixed feelings: 'Alas! it is but too true: the Queen is coming to pay me a visit at Stratfield Saye.' It was not often that royalty stayed with a commoner, and before the sovereign and her large retinue could be accommodated there were walls to be knocked down and rooms enlarged, servants' bells to be installed and extensive decorating to be carried out. All went well, despite a nervous housekeeper's pessimism, and the Duke was able to report: 'She [the Queen] was in perfect good Humour during the whole Time, very gracious to everybody; and everybody pleased.'

In 1851 the Duke's taste for novelty and his tireless interest in mechanical invention drew him to the Great Exhibition. Though his body might be frail and his step uncertain, his youthful spirit was delighted by that impressive display of Victorian technical achievement. As he wandered enthralled among the machinery and working models he was followed by admiring multitudes. He became, indeed, as much of a 'sight' as the Exhibition itself.

'Never did I see such a mob, or get such a rubbing, scrubbing and mashing . . .' he wrote. 'They rushed upon me from all directions – Men, Women, and Children, all collecting into a crowd and endeavouring to touch me!' He had lately been appointed Ranger of Hyde Park, and so the lofty glass building which housed the Exhibition came under his charge. Unfortunately the exhibits were being marred by the incursions of flocks of sparrows. No-one dared shoot them for fear of shattering the glass. In desperation the Queen herself sent for the Duke.

The victor of Waterloo had the answer. 'Try sparrowhawks, Ma'am,' he advised. She did. And henceforward the exhibits remained immaculate.

Next year, on May Day, he celebrated his eighty-third birthday. When on horseback he swayed alarmingly from side to side, and when on foot he tottered laboriously. Failing health made him irritable sometimes, and his Irish temper was apt to flare if well-meaning folk attempted to help him. An elderly servant, almost as shaky as the Duke, once gave him a leg up on to his saddle. The Duke shook him off in anger and grinned sardonically as the old fellow tumbled into the gutter. But he quickly repented his outbursts, and those around him loved him none the less.

In June there was the usual Waterloo Banquet, attended this time by Prince Albert, the only guest who had not been present at the battle. It was an evening full of memories. At the head of the table sat the Duke, heavy with honours and bowed with years. Between the sensitive, day-dreaming son of a minor noble family and the man who had become as much of an institution as the monarchy there stretched an incredible distance. He had travelled it thanks to an energy and a single-mindedness which had something almost monk-like about it. Despite the advantage his early aristocratic connections gave him, he would still not have risen so high without incessant hard work and determination to master each task as it presented itself. By his actions, which taught far more than any amount of preaching, he set an example that was adopted not by the Victorian age alone. His influence still permeates many of the traditions of military, administrative and social life.

No-one contributed more than the Duke to the peculiarly English concept of the 'gentleman'. The gentleman, as typified by the Duke, does not flaunt his emotions to the embarrassment of his companions. This does not mean, of course, that he is a man without feelings. The Duke had violent passions, but he taught himself to control them successfully, perhaps too successfully. Circumstances had frustrated his emotional life, and his deep capacity for affection was directed towards children, men who had fought with him, political colleagues who had been loyal to him, and the host of people, deserving or otherwise, to whom he gave freely of his charity. His enemies he contemplated without rancour, and it is impossible to think of him approving, as did Napoleon, of assassination.

Like Dr Johnson, the Duke was the embodiment of common-sense—a quality, after all, which is not so very common. Again like Johnson, he was a convinced Tory. It is unwise, however, to dismiss him as a mere reactionary. While he accepted the privileges his position gave him, he believed that he was only justified in doing so by fulfilling the far more important obligations it entailed. Whatever personal inconvenience there might be, he conceived of his duty as service to the country. He was never a good party politician, and his unsuccessful years as leader of the Tory Opposition were due to an honest—some would call it naïve—reluctance to hinder the workings of lawful government. He placed the public good above all else and offered the spectacle of service without the slightest flaw of ambition or self-seeking. He was, in the last resort, only human, and his occasional displays of vanity over the statues and pictures that were dedicated to him are set in their proper perspective by his comment to a friend: 'Perhaps there is no man now existing who would like to meet me on a field of battle; in that line I am superior. But when the war is over and the troops disbanded, what is your great general more than anybody else? . . . I am necessarily inferior to every man in his own line . . . I cannot saw or plane like a carpenter, or make shoes like a shoemaker, or understand cultivation like a farmer. Each of these, *on his own ground*, meets me on terms of superiority. I feel I am but a man.'

And so he dozed on at the last Waterloo Banquet in 1851. His young staff officers had become grey-headed generals now and they argued hotly over the details artists had put into pictures of the battle. The Duke was not very well up in art. Music was his forte. The warmest commendation of a battle picture he could offer was: 'Good – very good; not too much smoke!' The candles burnt low and trembled in the draught that eddied through the tall doorways. The last of the wine circulated round the long table, and one by one the veterans of Waterloo departed. The Duke made for bed. Perhaps, on the way, he stopped for a last look at his favourite Corregio: *The Agony in the Garden.* Although he never posed as an art lover, he knew what he liked. The picture was fitted with a sliding glass panel which he would unlock before gently dusting the canvas with a silk handkerchief. Then his head touched the pillow and he slept immediately. 'I don't like lying awake; it does no good,' he once said. 'I make a point never to lie awake.'

The leaves were yellowing when he travelled down to Walmer Castle that year. The family was there and he took long walks with his grandchildren on the ramparts. He went by train to Folkestone and visited an old friend, walking sturdily up and down hill for three miles to reach him. There was talk of the Irish problem, of the horse Copenhagen, and of 'my old Spanish infantry'. The Duke denied that he ever said 'Up Guards and at 'em!'

One morning among his voluminous correspondence, there was a letter from a madman reporting that he would call and deliver a message from the Lord next day. 'We shall see,' chuckled the Duke.

Two days later, on 14 September, he slept until seven o'clock. His valet pulled the curtains and told him it was late.

'Is it?' said the Duke heavily. 'Do you know where the apothecary lives?'

'Yes, your Grace.'

'Then send and let him know that I should like to see him. I don't feel quite well, and I will lie still till he comes.'

The apothecary was sent for and the Duke was lifted into a high-backed chair. He stared sightlessly out at the sea from his bare little room. In the evening a tearful gardener met a visitor at the drawbridge to the Castle. 'It is all over – he is gone,' he said.

The coffin was taken up to London and lay in state. The whole country went into mourning. A magnificent hearse was constructed measuring twenty-seven feet long. It took the shape of a vast and ornate pagoda embellished with laurel wreaths, sabres and dolphins beneath a silver-embroidered canopy. Drawn by twelve black horses loaded with plumes, the cumbersome vehicle rolled on its iron wheels into the Mall. Behind it walked a horse bearing an empty saddle and the field-marshal's boots reversed. Guns boomed every minute from the Park and the roll of muffled kettle-drums surged rhythmically as the procession wound through streets puddled with November rainstorms. Long columns of soldiers from every regiment of the British Army, Chelsea Pensioners and cohorts of wailing bagpipes marched to the sombre melody of the Dead March in *Saul*. They were watched by bare-headed crowds numbering more than one and a half million. As a spectacle it was the most breath-taking the century had ever witnessed.

Wrote Queen Victoria: 'He was the GREATEST man this country ever produced, and the most devoted and loyal subject and the staunchest supporter the Crown ever had.' Fulsome and excessive were the obituaries, grand and glorious was the funeral ceremony whose pomp the Duke would certainly have deplored. The most fitting epitaph had already been pronounced by Kitty twenty years before, as she lay on her deathbed at Apsley House. Raising herself up and pointing to all the victory trophies presented to him by grateful kings and countries, she sighed weakly: 'All tributes to merit, there's the value, no corruption ever suspected even. . . .' When all is said and done, his Duchess may not have been such a fool as he and his friends thought she was.

# Suggestions for further reading

The most important sources of information about Wellington are to be found in: *The Despatches of Field Marshal the Duke of Wellington*, edited by Lieutenant-Colonel Gurwood (12 vols., John Murray, 1834–1838); in *The General Orders of Field Marshal the Duke of Wellington*, edited by Lieutenant-Colonel Gurwood (Clowes, 1837); and in *Supplementary Despatches and Memoranda of Field Marshal Arthur, Duke of Wellington, K.G.* (15 vols., John Murray, 1858). As, however, these publications are hard to find except in museums and large libraries, the following list of books, restricted to those published in English, will be of interest. Those marked with an asterisk are particularly useful as they contain long extracts from the Duke's correspondence and other writings.

Aldington, Richard. *Wellington*. Heinemann, 1946

Brett-James, A. (Editor). *Wellington at War, 1794–1815*. Macmillan, 1961

Creevey, Thomas. (Ed. Sir Herbert Maxwell). *The Creevey Papers*. 2 vols., John Murray, 1903

Croker, J. W. (Ed. L. J. Jennings). *The Croker Papers*. 3 vols. John Murray, 1884

Gleig, J. W. *Life of Arthur, Duke of Wellington*. Everyman. (First published in 1873)

Guedalla, Philip. *The Duke*. Hodder & Stoughton, 1931

Herold, J. Christopher. *The Battle of Waterloo*. Cassells, 1967

Hickey, W. (Ed. Alfred Spencer). *Memoirs of William Hickey*. 4 vols., Hurst & Blackett, 1925

Howard, Michael (Editor). *Wellingtonian Studies*. Gale & Polden, 1959

Maxwell, Sir Herbert. *The Life of Wellington*. 2 vols., Sampson Low Marston & Co., 1899

Maxwell, W. H. *Life of Field Marshal His Grace The Duke of Wellington*. 3 vols., H. H. Bailey & Co., 1839–1841

Mercer, General Cavalié. *Journal of the Waterloo Campaign (1870)*. Peter Davies, 1927

Napier, Sir W. F. P. *History of the War in the Peninsula*. 6 vols., Thos. & William Boone, 1851

Oman, C. W. C. *Wellington's Army, 1809–1814*. Edward Arnold, 1913

Oman, Sir Charles. *A History of the Peninsular War*. 7 vols., Oxford University Press, 1902–1930

Petrie, Sir Charles. *Wellington. A Reassessment*. James Barrie, 1956

Stanhope, 5th Earl. *Notes on Conversations with the Duke of Wellington, 1831–1851*. (First publ., 1888). Oxford University Press, 1938

Ward, S. G. P. *Wellington*. Batsford, 1963

*ibid. Wellington's Headquarters*. Oxford University Press, 1957

Weller, Jac. *Wellington in the Peninsula*. Nicholas Vane, 1962

Wellesley, Muriel. *The Man Wellington*. Constable, 1937

*ibid.* *Wellington in Civil Life*. Constable, 1939

Wellington, 7th Duke of. (formerly Lord Gerald Wellesley). *Wellington and His Friends*. Macmillan, 1965

*ibid.* *The Conversations of the First Duke of Wellington with G. W. Chad*. St Nicholas Press, 1956

*ibid.* *A Selection from the Private Correspondence of the First Duke of Wellington*. Roxburghe Club, 1952

*ibid.* (with John Steegmann). *The Iconography of the First Duke of Wellington*. Dent, 1935

26. *The Duke of Wellington.*   *(A daguerrotype in the collection of Anthony Denney.)*

# Summary of events

**1769:** May 1 Arthur Wellesley born in Dublin

**1782–4:** Eton

**1786:** Brussels

**1787:** Gazetted as ensign; becomes aide-de-camp to the Lord-Lieutenant of Ireland. M.P. for Trim in the Irish Parliament
Lieutenant

**1789:** Fall of the Bastille

**1791:** Captain

**1793:** Major
Lieutenant-Colonel
Revolutionary armies sweep Europe. Wellesley sails to support the Duke of York at Ostend
Battle of Boxtel, Brabant. Wellesley's first battle

**1796:** Sails for India

**1797:** May. Richard Wellesley arrives as Governor General of India.
Arthur marches to meet Tippoo Sahib

**1799:** April. Seringapatam
Arthur appointed Governor of Mysore

**1802:** April. Promoted to Major-General
Mahratta Wars: Siege of Ahmednuggar; Battle of Assaye; Dec. 15 taking of Gawilghur
Knighted

**1805:** Spring. Resigns and returns to England
Calls at St Helena on return journey
Battle of Austerlitz. Austria falls to Napoleon

**1806:** Spring. Marries Kitty Pakenham
Tilsit. Napoleon's pact with the Tsar
Richard Wellesley resigns Governor Generalship of India and returns to England.
Sir Arthur M.P. for Rye
Chief Secretary for Ireland
Leads expedition to capture the Danish fleet at Copenhagen
Joseph Bonaparte proclaimed King of Spain. Napoleon sends expeditionary force to Portugal

**1808:** June. A Spanish representative comes to England and asks for help
June 14 Sir Arthur (Lieutenant-General) put in command of Peninsular forces
Resigns Chief Secretaryship mid-July. Embarks for Portugal
Aug. 17 Roliça; Vimeiro; Convention of Cintra
Sir Arthur returns to England and his post as Irish Secretary
Napoleon renews attack on Spain

**1809:** Jan. 16 Death of Sir John Moore at Corunna
Sir Arthur back in Portugal, Oporto mid-July. Spanish campaign opens at Talavera
Sir Arthur created Viscount Wellington of Talavera

**1810:** July. Almeida surrenders to Napoleon
Torres Vedras

**1811:** Jan. 17 Ciudad Rodrigo
Created Earl
April 6. Badajoz

**1812:** June. Wins Salamanca and enters Madrid
Created Marquess
Autumn. Fails to take Burgos
Napoleon's retreat from Moscow

**1813:** June 21 Vitoria
Field Marshal
Seige of San Sebastian, enters France

**1814:** March 12 Enters Bordeaux
Defeats Soult at Toulouse. End of Peninsular War
Abdication of Napoleon: exiled to Elba
Wellington returns to London in triumph. Created Duke
British Ambassador to France
Winter. Present at Congress of Vienna

**1815:** March. Napoleon escapes from Elba
The Allied armies assemble near Brussels
June 18. Waterloo
July. Napoleon surrenders. The 100 Days over. Sent to St Helena. Wellington takes up command of the Army of Occupation
Restoration of Louis XVIII

**1818:** Winter. Returns to England
Enters Lord Liverpool's Government

**1820:** The Cato St Conspiracy

**1821:** George IV.
Britain's representative at the Congress of Vienna

**1826:** Mission to Tsar at St Petersburg
April. Canning Prime Minister
Wellington resigns

**1827:** Jan. Wellington instructed to form a government

**1829:** Repeal of the Test Act
Government falls in battle over Reform

**1830:** Revolution in France

**1831:** April. Death of Kitty, Duchess of Wellington
Installed as Chancellor of Oxford University

**1832:** Passing of the Reform Bill
Appointed Lord Warden of Cinque Ports
Temporarily leads government before Peel takes up position

**1837:** Victoria

**1838:** Prepares to defend London against the Chartist riots

**1851:** The Great Exhibition
Sept. 14 Dies

27. *Wellington's funeral procession passing Apsley House, from the engraving by Picken, 1852.*
(*By permission of the Victoria and Albert Museum.*)